The switchboard operator knows your name, the people at the desk say welcome back when you come through the door, and they try to give you your favorite room if you've stayed there a long time, and it's fine to have dinner in the dining room if you're there alone. My *favorite is the* Hotel Bel Air *because that's where* I *spent my honeymoon . . .We all know small hotels are sexy because they are small and intimate.*

—Helen Gurley Brown

A *small hotel is your home away from home.*

—Caroline Hunt Schoellkopf

One of the rewards of designing small high quality hotels is that they often are the culmination of a greater sense of interest from the owner and the operator, and therefore provide us, the designer, with a more personalized direction. It *also offers us an opportunity to promote the specialized field of hotel design to a higher level of professionalism and excellence. This in turn influences the level of sophistication and appreciation of the general public who previously experienced this design only in high end residential work.*

—James Northcutt

ELEGANT
SMALL HOTELS
A CONNOISSEUR'S GUIDE

PAMELA LANIER

Published by:
John Muir Publications, Inc.
P.O. Box 613
Santa Fe, NM 87504

Design and production by Mary Shapiro.
Typeset by Copygraphics, Santa Fe, New Mexico.
Cover photographs of The Mansion on Turtle Creek by Jaime Ardiles-Arce, used by permission from Rosewood Hotels, Inc.

Library of Congress Catalogue No. 86-42877

ISBN 0-912528-57-5

First Edition September 1986
Second Printing October 1986

Book trade distributor:
W. W. Norton & Co., Inc.
New York, NY

Printed in the United States of America

This book is lovingly dedicated to the memory of John Muir.

This guidebook is the result of the talent, energy, style and taste of many people. First, special thanks to Marianne Barth and Katherine Bertolucci, whose help made this guide possible; to Ken Luboff, a man of many talents and lots of good ideas; to Richard Harris (one great editor!); to Judy Cash, idea lady; and to Mary Shapiro, whose exquisite taste has infused this project from the beginning.

Special thanks also to Lauren Childress, Venetia Young, Mary Kreuger, Jay Clark, Marjorie Silverman, Harriet Choice, Jeremy Dove, Frank Waldrop, Sartain Lanier and Carol Delattre.

All information in this book is subject to change without notice. We strongly recommend that you call ahead and always verify the information in this book before making final plans or reservations. The author and publisher cannot be held responsible for inaccurate or out of date information.

"There's a small hotel,
with a wishing well,
I *wish that we were there*
together . . ."
—Rodgers and Hart

CONTENTS

INTRODUCTION

. . . And then there was the time that my band (eight men and one woman) and myself travelled all day changing planes twice to get from New York to a small town in the west where we had to play that night. It had been *that* kind of travelling day—replete with rudeness, abruptness, computer mixups and a complete lack of attention or care for the individual. So somehow it didn't really surprise us when we found upon reaching our ultimate destination that all our instruments and other bags had been mis-routed and sent to Kalamazoo, Chattanooga or some other strange Indian-sounding city. This meant that only those of us who had carried our clothes on board (something I've learned to do) had anything to wear that evening and only me on piano (it doesn't travel with us, thank God) and the trumpet player (who had carried his instrument with him) had anything to play that night—a most unlikely duet! What to do? One could rage uselessly at the cipher in back of the airlines desk, or one could attempt to be cunning.

Opting for the second alternative, I remembered that we were staying in an elegant small hotel which had a reputation for service and attention to the individual; so with fading hope I called the hotel. I was immediately switched to a polite concierge whom I belabored with our seemingly insoluble problem. He listened attentively, asked intelligent questions (a first that day, I'll tell you) and told me to come directly to the hotel and see him there. When we arrived and assembled numbly around his desk, we found that this wonderful man had done the following: he had contacted the local music store which was standing by to hear the specifications of the instruments we needed and would deliver them to the job on time; he had contacted the local evening wear store which was waiting to hear our sizes and would deliver to the hotel; he had contacted the airlines and traced our bags; he had pre-registered us in our rooms; and finally, he had set up a private room for us in which he had arranged to serve us dinner before we left for the job. Furthermore it all worked.

Believe me, I need no further inducement to stay in elegant small hotels for the rest of my days. When I travel, which I do a great deal of the time (we played in 41 states in the last three years), I really do appreciate those wonderful qualities which can be found in these hotels: politeness, attentiveness and really an old-fashioned attention to detail and to the needs of the client. Sadly, these qualities are quite lacking in everyday life as we prepare for the 21st century. I'm glad to see, though, that these hotels are returning to a sense of service and style. . . I just hope that with the publication of this book my band and I will be able to get reservations whenever we need them!

—*Peter Duchin*

GUIDENOTES

If you are among those discerning travelers who understand that the essence of the good life is quality, this book has been designed especially to enhance your travel enjoyment.

To identify the most elegant small hotels in the United States today, we have used the following criteria:

When we say "small," we mean fewer than 200 guest rooms; in fact, the typical hotel selected for inclusion in this guide has approximately one-half that number. We have found that small hotels are best able to offer the high staff-to-guest ratio enabling a genuine concern for each guest's comfort and pleasure.

By "elegant," we mean decor—and also something more. If a hotel is to be one's "home away from home," its atmosphere should be like that of a fine residence. The feeling should be reflected not only in design, color and furnishings, but also in those little touches that *really* matter: fresh flowers, nightly turn-down (with a chocolate!), overnight shoeshine, luxurious toiletries and oversized towels. . . all the myriad details that add up to the intangible quality we call elegance.

For us to even consider a particular hotel, it must first have met the foregoing standards. Other factors we have kept in mind while separating the exceptional from the merely first-class relate to individual travelers' needs. For example. . .

If you conduct business while traveling, such facilities as secretarial service on call, teleconferencing, telex and computer telecommunications, and perhaps an appropriately-sized meeting or conference room, will be essential.

If you are among the growing number of people to whom physical fitness is a personal must, your hotel should provide in-house facilities such as swimming pool, tennis, spa and massage room, and perhaps weight training equipment. Many of our recommended hotels also arrange guest privileges at prestigious private country clubs and health centers.

If you are among those travelers for whom fine cuisine is a top priority, we agree completely. We have chosen our hotels with excellent dining in mind, and we often include a description of a representative dinner we have enjoyed recently at the hotel. The words "Dress Code" in any listing show that coat and tie are appropriate; where a hotel's dining room is guests-only, not open to the general public, this fact is also indicated.

Whether you travel for business, pleasure, or a bit of both, each elegant small hotel described in this guide deserves a special place in your plans and your memories.

This guide encompasses four types of elegant hotel accommodations:

Grand Luxe Hotels: Each of these world-class hotels projects an incomparable aura of tradition and grace. A few of the services provided are full concierge staff, superb restaurant and room service, an attentive but very discreet staff and a sumptuous atmosphere of well-secured luxury. There are only about 3 dozen such hotels in the United States.

City Center Hotels: Designed especially for the executive traveler, each of these hotels offers a comfortable, inviting environment where he or she may return each day to lodgings ideally appointed to satisfy business, personal and recreational needs. Special emphasis is placed upon conference facilities and services for executives.

Outstanding Resorts: The quick weekend trip or brief resort holiday is becoming the new vacation style of the ultra-busy. From a wide range of possibilities, we have selected our resort recommendations with regard for their luxurious ambience, excellent cuisine and sporting facilities. Most also offer excellent conference facilities and are perfect for combining recreation and business meetings in beautiful surroundings.

Affordable Elegance: Though one normally expects elegant lodgings to come at higher-than-ordinary rates, we have discovered a select few that offer the best of both worlds: comfortable, elegantly appointed rooms, with excellent restaurants, access to sports facilities and complete business services, and most essential amenities associated with Grand Luxe hotel—at surprisingly reasonable prices.

For different styles in "affordable elegance," please check our most recent edition of *The Complete Guide to Bed & Breakfasts, Inns and Guesthouses in the United States and Canada* by Pamela Lanier (also from John Muir Publications, available in fine bookstores everywhere).

We have indicated room rates with a code showing the price range of the lowest-priced double-occupancy room:
$ = From $50 to 100
$$ = From $100 to 150
$$$ = From $150 to 225
$$$$ = From $225 up

An asterisk (*) following the price code indicates that quite outstanding suites, are also available from $300 up.

All prices quoted are European Plan; a few resorts offer the American Plan, and some others provide complimentary continental breakfast. Be sure to call to verify exact prices when making your reservation.

We have noted many amenities provided. Other services and sundries are often available. When you call to book reservations, ask whether the hotel offers those you desire.

We have noted when a hotel will not accept pets, or when pets are accepted only under special conditions. An additional deposit is often required. In establishments that do not permit pets, the concierge can make arrangements with the best local kennel.

Children are accepted when accompanied by their parents except where otherwise noted. There is no additional charge for children under a certain age, which varies among hotels.

Most hotels have at least some rooms designed to accommodate the handicapped. We have noted the number of rooms so equipped. Hotels with only a few handicapped-accessible rooms should be booked well in advance.

An important key to getting the most out of your Elegant Small Hotel experience is to allow the concierge to assist you whenever possible. The hotels described in this guide are small enough to permit a degree of personal attention rarely encountered in modern life. Accordingly, the function of the concierge is to cater to the individual needs (and whims) of each guest. Rather than attempt a detailed description of services and amenities the concierge can arrange—which would leave no space in this guide for the hotels themselves—we have presented in full "A Concierge's Day," the viewpoint of one outstanding concierge, on the following page.

Every attempt has been made to provide absolutely current information. Some information contained in this guide has been provided by the hotels' management, and management policies may change. If you feel that anything in this book is even slightly inaccurate, please inform us so we can put it right in future editions.

We appreciate reader comments, including any hotel we have overlooked which you feel deserves to be included.

—*Pamela Lanier* —September 1986

A CONCIERGE'S DAY

"I am absolutely certain we can have the car and driver here in twenty minutes, sir. I only need to know what sort of car and what sort of driver you would prefer. And yes, I expect your day in the wine country will be splendid; the weather is perfect."

The 20-minute wait for the special car and driver to arrive will not be wasted. The concierge first calls ahead for luncheon reservations at a spot that normally requires two weeks' notice. Next, he will call the wineries for any special considerations that might be possible for his guest. After all, everything must be the best. (It will soon become evident that perfect weather is the only thing the concierge has *not* arranged—the sunshine being courtesy of a somewhat higher power).

The larger day's work begins for the concierge at this small Nob Hill hotel in San Francisco with a review of the arriving guest list and of their special requests noted in his log. He opens that delicious document with the same excitement felt by a maestro opening the score of a beautiful symphony.

Appreciating that not everyone who travels in America is yet fully acquainted with the full range of services he can provide, the concierge will promptly call each guest within minutes of arrival to extend a personal introduction and a warm invitation to take full advantage of his skills and resources. To him and his hotel, every guest is a Very Important Person.

The concierge next turns his attention to a couple at his desk, eager to begin a day of sightseeing. Shopping, museum hopping and general about-towning are the plan, with a lovely lunch along the way. The concierge will not only point them in the right direction but also enhance their day with helpful hints and local insights.

The couple will return with happy faces and tired feet, to swap a few stories with the concierge and then retire for a nap or workout followed by tea.

Afterward they will consult the concierge once again to plan an evening grand finale to a delight-filled day. Knowledgable and sensitive to his territory, he can advise them concerning matters of cuisine, attire, entertainment, transportation and adventure; then he will make the necessary arrangements.

You see, living vicariously is the route to concierge heaven. As the concierge plans the guests' daytime and evening activities with them, striving to maximize their pleasure, and as he takes the necessary measures to bring the plan to reality, and as he hears guests tell of their experiences afterwards, he feels something beyond professional pride. He actually enjoys it.

—*Jeremy Dove*

[*Mr. Dove, Concierge at* The Huntington *in* San Francisco, *has graciously contributed the foregoing on behalf of himself and his fellow members of the professional concierge association* Les Clefs d'Or USA, Ltd. *And special thanks to* Marjorie Silverman, *First* Vice *President of* Les Clefs d'Or, *for her help on this project.* —P.L.]

THE BOULDERS

Address: P.O. Box 2090, 34631 N. Tom Darlington Rd., Carefree 85377
Phone No.: 602-488-9009
Reservation Services: Rockresorts, New York: 800-223-7637
Rates: $$$*
Credit Cards: Visa, MC, DC, AmEx
No. of Rooms: 120
Services and Amenities: Gift shop, Valet service, Avis car rental, Tennis and golf pro shops, Laundry, Complimentary newspaper, Cable TV, Telephone, Robes, Sun lamps, Shampoo, Conditioner, Soaps
Restrictions: No pets; handicapped access to 5 rooms
Concierge: 8:00 a.m. to 6:00 p.m.
Room Service: Continental breakfast only
Restaurant: Latilla Room, 7:00-10:00 a.m., 12:00-2:30 p.m., 6:00-9:00 p.m., Dress Code; Palo Verde Room, 11:30 a.m.-2:00 p.m., 6:00-9:30 p.m.
Bar: Discovery Lounge
Business Facilities: Copiers, Audio-visual
Conference Rooms: 1, capacity-200, theatre style; 3 executive conference rooms
Sports Facilities: 6 plexi-cushion tennis courts, 3 nine-hole golf courses, 2 heated swimming pools, whirlpool
Location: 15 miles northeast of Phoenix
Attractions: Shopping-2 miles; Day trips to Sedona/Oak Creek Canyon, Fly or tour Grand Canyon, February—Parada del Sol and Arabian Horse Show

The Boulders, fifteen miles northeast of Phoenix, is the newest Rockresort. The architecture by Bob Bacon incorporates adobe walls and natural flagstone in harmony with the natural beauty of the surrounding Sonoran desert foothills. Navajo rugs and southwestern Indian pottery accent the subtle desert-hued decor.

120 individual casitas are scattered throughout the 1,300-acre resort. Rooms have viga ceilings, horno-style corner fireplaces, private patios and such special touches as quality toiletries and fluffy bathrobes.

Outdoor sports abound: 27 holes of golf designed by Jay Morrish, 6 plexi-cushioned all-weather tennis courts, 2 swimming pools, hot tubs and a fine riding stable nearby. The concierge will gladly arrange a hot air balloon ride, desert jeep trip or spectacular flying tour of the Grand Canyon.

Three dining rooms offer a full range of outstanding cuisine. The Latilla has regional specialty menus as well as a diverse and tantalizing main menu and irresistable continental pastries; it also affords a stunning view of waterfalls and the impressive rock formations for which the resort is named. The light and airy Palo Verde Room features Rockresort favorites including rack of lamb and prime rib, and southwestern and Mexican dining specialties.

Executive casitas are available for private business meetings, and the nearly 2,000-square-foot ballroom can accommodate larger conferences and seminars.

ARIZONA INN

Walkways meandering through 14 acres of lawn and lush gardens create the feel of a desert oasis in a quiet residential neighborhood near the University of Arizona. The charming Majorcan Spanish-style structures, built in 1930, are of pink adobe with blue shutters and trim.

Each guest room is individually decorated. All have spacious 1930s-style bathrooms with white octagonal tile flooring, and most have private patios or balconies. All furniture in the rooms has been handmade by veterans.

Fine dining is available in the formal Arizona Inn dining room. A delicious dinner might consist of canapes, an iced relish tray, filet of sole with admiral sauce, a hot consomme au porto, rack of lamb with fresh mint sauce and vegetable bouquetiere. To complete the feast, you may choose from a tempting selection of pastries.

The cocktail lounge has a garden decor with hanging plants, Audubon prints on the walls, and luxuriously upholstered furnishings. Guests congregate in the library, where a crackling evening fire highlights ornate Moroccan and Afghanistani rugs.

The 60-foot swimming pool with adjoining wading pool is sheltered on all sides. There are two Har-Tru (clay) tennis courts, and guests are extended privileges to several private golf clubs. This is an excellent conference location, with facilities for 4 to 255 persons.

Address: 2200 E. Elm St., Tucson 85719
Phone No.: 602-325-1541
Toll Free Cable: 800-421-1093
Telex: 165523 AZ Inn TUC
Rates: $
Credit Cards: AmEx, Visa, MC
No. of Rooms: 85
Suites: 8
Services and Amenities: Valet service, Library, Parking, Car hire, House doctor on call, Laundry, Baby-sitting service, TV, Radio
Restrictions: Handicapped access to 5 rooms
Concierge: Exec. Secty/Bell Desk, 7:00 a.m.-10:00 p.m.
Room Service: 7:00-11:00 a.m., 11:30 a.m.-9:00 p.m.
Restaurant: Arizona Inn Dining Room, Dress Code during winter season
Bar: Arizona Inn Cocktail Lounge, Mon.-Sat. 11:00 a.m.-Midnight, Sun. Noon-Midnight
Business Facilities: Message center, Copiers, Telex, Other business services arranged.
Conference Rooms: 4, capacity 225
Sports Facilities: 2 Har-Tru (clay) tennis courts, Croquet, Swimming pool
Location: 3 mi. Speedway E. Campbell N. Elm E., 12 mi. from airport, 3 mi. from I-10
Attractions: Arizona-Sonora Desert Museum 12 mi., San Xavier Mission 12 mi., Old Tucson movie location 10 mi.

THE CAPITAL HOTEL

Address: 111 W. Markham St., Little Rock 72201
Phone No.: 501-374-7474
Toll-Free Cable: 800-643-6456
Reservation Service: Princess Hotels, 800-228-0808
Rates: $
Credit Cards: AmEx, Visa, MC, DC
No. of Rooms: 123
Suites: 5
Services and Amenities: Gift shop, Valet service, Baby-sitting service, Valet parking garage, Laundry, TV, Radio, Robes, Soap, Shampoo, Shoehorn, Shower cap
Restrictions: Small pets-must not be left alone in room; handicapped access to 6 rooms
Room Service: 6:30 a.m.-11:00 p.m.
Restaurant: Ashley's Restaurant, 6:30 a.m.-10:30 a.m., 11:30 a.m.-2:30 p.m., 6:00-11:00 p.m.
Bar: The Capital Bar, Mon.-Fri. 11:30-1:00 a.m., Sat. 11:30 a.m.-Midnight
Business Facilities: Secretarial service, Translators, Copiers, Audio-visual, Telex
Conference Rooms: 5, capacity 100
Location: Downtown
Attractions: Walking distance to Old State House, Territorial Restoration and Riverfront Park

When former President Ulysses S. Grant stayed here in 1880, reporters described The Capital Hotel as "one of the finest edifices in the South." Newly restored in 1983 and listed on the National Register of Historic Places, the hotel retains Old South elegance in the lobby's faux marble columns and grand staircase, the 1907 stained-glass skylight above the atrium, and Victorian decorative moldings throughout.

The 123 spacious guest rooms and suites feature 15-foot ceilings, oversized arched windows and authentic decor in the style of a century ago. Suites offer king-sized four-poster beds and carved oak tables with marble tops.

Ashley's, the hotel's formal dining room, is famed throughout the mid-South for fresh seafood and regional specialties served with a continental flair. Enjoy, for example, an appetizer of Oysters Ashley followed by Veal Gulfport and profiterolles. The Capital Bar, with its dark lustrous hardwood trim, chandeliers and overstuffed settees, is a popular meeting place for Arkansas' government and business leaders.

Conference facilities range from intimate old-fashioned parlors to the 1480-square-foot Watkins Lounge adjoining the mezzanine balcony. For formal receptions, Ashley's provides delectable hors d'oeuvres such as imported cheeses and fresh fruits served on decorated mirrors and Alaskan crab claws displayed on hand-carved ice.

In Little Rock's historic district, The Capital Hotel is within easy walking distance of the state capitol complex and the city's modern convention center.

L'ERMITAGE

"Outside it's Beverly Hills . . . Inside it's Europe," L'Ermitage proclaims, and this *hotel de grande classe* lives up to its motto. Even by the standards of America's most glamorous community, the Old World ambience here is truly special.

Continental hospitality abounds. After complimentary continental breakfast, guests may wish to make visits within Beverly Hills via one of the hotel's private chauffeur-driven limousines, or sunbathe amid fragrant flowers and lush greenery in the roof gardens by the swimming pool and whirlpool spa. The bar serves complimentary pate and caviar to the accompaniment of classical piano from 5 to 7 p.m. Attention to guests' comfort includes twice-daily maid service with evening turndown.

Each of the 114 suites is individually decorated in soft pastel tones, with fireplace, private balcony and fresh flowers in the living room. Original artwork graces the walls.

The elegant Cafe Russe is exclusively for hotel guests' intimate dining. If you prefer to dine *en suite*, 24-hour room service is available.

A full health club and tennis court are nearby at sister hotels Mondrian and Le Parc. The boutiques and bistros of Rodeo Drive are just a short stroll from the front portal of L'Ermitage.

Address: 9291 Burton Way, Beverly Hills 90210
Phone No.: 213-278-3344, 800-424-4443
Telex: 698441 BVHL
Rates: $$$*
Credit Cards: AmEx, Visa, MC, DC, CB
No. of Suites: 114
Services and Amenities: Laundry, Valet service, Parking, Car hire, Complimentary shoeshine, House Doctor on call, Baby-sitting service, Complimentary newspaper, Cable TV, Radio, Telephone, Robes, Custom milled soap and personal care products
Restrictions: Pets with approval and deposit; no handicapped access
Concierge: 7:00 a.m.-11:00 p.m.
Room Service: 24 hours
Restaurant: Cafe Russe, 7:00 a.m.-11:00 p.m., Guests only, Dress Code
Bar: The Bar, 11:00 a.m.-1:00 a.m.
Business Facilities: Message center, Secretarial services on call, Copiers, Audio-visual on request, Telex
Conference Rooms: 2, capacity 60
Sports Facilities: Heated swimming pool, whirlpool
Location: Residential Beverly Hills
Attractions: Near Rodeo Dr., Century City and UCLA

VENTANA INN

Address: Highway 1, Big Sur 93920
Phone Nos.: 404-667-2331, 408-624-4812
Toll-free Cable: CA 800-628-6500
Rates: $$
Credit Cards: Visa, AmEx, DC, MC
No. of Rooms: 40 **Suites:** 4
Services and Amenities: Parking, Complimentary newspaper, TV, Video cassette player, Radio
Restrictions: No pets; children discouraged; handicapped access to 6 rooms
Room Service: Continental breakfast 8:00-10:00 a.m.; Wine and beer, 8:00 a.m.-11:00 p.m.
Restaurant: Ventana, (lunch) weekdays Noon-3:00 p.m., weekends 11:00 a.m.-3:45 p.m., 6:00 p.m.-9:00 p.m.
Bar: Ventana, 11:00 a.m.-Midnight
Business Facilities: Message center, Partial secretarial service, Spanish translators, Copiers, Audio-visual
Conference Rooms: 1, capacity 40
Sports Facilities: Hiking, riding, whirlpool, sauna, massage, swimming pool
Location: Highway 1, Big Sur
Attractions: Wilderness and ocean

Bordered by rugged canyons and a 40-acre redwood grove overlooking the breathtaking Big Sur coast, this Inn succeeds in harmonizing luxurious accommodations with stunning natural beauty. 163 miles south of San Francisco and only 63 miles from San Simeon, with boundless Pacific views, abundant wildlife, and the Santa Lucia Mountains as a backdrop, Ventana is an idyllic spot for a peaceful, relaxing escape.

Forty rooms and townhouse suites are nestled amid the 243 pristine acres. The buildings, by designer-artist Kipp Stewart, are of weathered cedar. The interior has been designed by Courtney Bruhn in a palette of pastel blues, pinks and gold, to create a light, open, country feeling.

Every room has a private balcony or patio, most with ocean views. Some have private hot tubs. In-room amenities include canopy beds, handmade quilts and luxurious linens.

The restaurant is internationally acclaimed for its California cuisine. Luncheon specialties include artichokes stuffed with crab and shrimp and served with a coarse-ground mustard sauce, and grilled skirt steak with salsa. Among the dinner offerings are a watercress goat cheese nicoise olive salad, grilled baby salmon in a Rose Beurre Blanc, and grilled fresh young chicken served in a raspberry vinegar and honey sauce. The on-premises French Bakery provides a fabulous array of pastries and tortes. The wine list is extensive and features not only outstanding California wines but also French and German wines and champagnes.

The outdoor dining terrace offers a panoramic 50-mile vista of the Pacific, while the paneled cedar-and-glass dining room has both ocean and mountain views.

Among the recreation facilities available are a 90-foot swimming pool and a bathhouse containing Japanese hot baths, hot tubs and sauna. Massage, facials and manicures are available. There is ample countryside for hiking, with easy acess to the beaches and State parks.

The premises offer no children's activities or child-care facilities; the management emphasizes that this resort is designed for adults seeking calm, peaceful natural surroundings.

THE HIGHLANDS INN

Sunset over the Pacific, viewed from the historic Grand Lodge promenade, is awesome. Waves crash on rocky crags 200 feet below, evening breezes whisper among Monterey pines, and whales break the surface of an ocean sparkling orange and indigo. The panorama has made The Highlands Inn a favorite writers' and artists' hideaway for 50 years.

The Grand Lodge was entirely renovated in 1985. The lobby area now features deep leather settees, backgammon boards, granite fireplaces and an antique grand piano.

New cottage-like suites and townhouses, as well as three open air hot tubs, are secluded along flowering walkways on the Inn's forested hillsides. Rooms feature natural wool Berber carpets, Italian linen-covered furniture, woodburning fireplaces and vista decks.

The Pacific's Edge Restaurant offers California gourmet cuisine such as ceviche in papaya, calamari with Gilroy elephant garlic, mosaic of sole and salmon with sauce watercress, and a dessert medley of fruit sorbets—with a 270 degree view of the rugged coastline.

The delights of the Monterey-Carmel area are close at hand, and the concierge will be happy to assist in planning sporting activities, entertainment and sightseeing tours. Many guests, however, spend romantic weekends here without leaving the inn's own fabulous grounds.

Address: P.O. Box 1700, Carmel 93921
Phone No.: 408-624-3801
Toll-free Cable: CA 800-682-4811
Reservation Services: VIP Reservations of Palo Alto, 415-474-5128
Rates: $$$*
Credit Cards: All major credit cards (AmEx for deposit only)
No. of Rooms: 145 **Suites:** 103
Services and Amenities: Gift shop in California Market, Valet service, Garage and parking, Car hire off-site, Baby-sitting service, Laundry, Complimentary local newspaper,, Cable TV, VCR available to rent, Radio, Telephone, Robes, Whirlpool bath, Soap, Shampoo, Bath gel
Restrictions: No pets; handicapped access to 6 rooms
Concierge: Thur.-Mon. 10:00 a.m.-6:00 p.m.
Room Service: 7:00 a.m.-10:00 p.m.
Restaurant: Pacific's Edge, 7:00-10:30 a.m., 11:30 a.m.-2:00 p.m., 6:00 p.m.-10.00 p.m. California market, 11:00 a.m.-11:00 p.m. daily
Bar: Sunset Lounge & The Tavern-11:00 a.m. to closing time
Business Facilities: Message Center, Secretarial Service, Translators, Copiers, Audio-visual, Telex
Conference Rooms: 6, capacity 170
Sports Facilities: Swimming pool
Location: Carmel Highlands
Attractions: Monterey Wine Country Tours, Point Lobos State reserve, Pebble Beach; 17-Mile Drive; Monterey Bay Aquarium, Cannery Row, Laguna Seca Raceway-Monterey Jazz Festival.

LA PLAYA

Address: Camino Real & Eighth, Carmel 93921
Phone No.: 408-624-6476
Toll-free: 800-582-8900
Rates: $
Credit Cards: Visa, MC, AmEx
No. of Rooms: 75 **Suites:** 2
Services and Amenities: Laundry, Free parking, House doctor, Baby-sitting service, Cable TV, Radio, Shampoo, 2 soaps, Shower caps, Bath gel, Hairdryers
Restrictions: No pets; handicapped access to 3 rooms
Concierge: Sun.-Thur. 8:00 a.m.-4:00 p.m., Fri.-Sat. 8:00 a.m.-8:00 p.m.
Room Service: 7:00 a.m.-11:00 p.m.
Restaurant: Spyglass Restaurant, 7:00-10:30 a.m., 11:30 a.m.-2:00 p.m., 5:00-10:00 p.m.
Bar: Spyglass Lounge, 10:00 a.m.-Midnight
Business Facilities: Message center, Secretarial service, Translators, Copiers, Audio-visual
Conference Rooms: 3, capacity 10-125
Sports Facilities: Heated outdoor swimming pool
Location: Residential Carmel Village
Attractions: 2 blocks to beach, shopping; 17-Mile Drive, Pt. Lobos, Carmel Mission, Monterey Bay Aquarium; 11 nearby golf courses

The "grand lady of Carmel-by-the-sea," as local residents have known this Mediterranean-style villa since artist Chris Jorgensen built it for his bride in 1904, is now grander than ever. A resort since the 1920s, La Playa was acquired in 1983 by the Cope family (owners of San Francisco's incomparable Huntington), who have done extensive restoration and renovation to make it Carmel's only full-service resort.

The subtly exquisite decor accents pale pastel walls and upholstery with custom hand-loomed area rugs, paintings by contemporary artists, and the Cope family's extensive collection of California antiques and heirlooms. Rooms afford views of the garden, the ocean, or residential Carmel. Handcrafted furnishings incorporate La Playa's mermaid motif in hues of soft rose and blue. The baths have marble floors and inlaid decorative tile.

The Spy Glass restaurant's gorgeous terrace is a perfect spot to watch the sunset. The wood-paneled interior of the restaurant provides a cozy dining atmosphere amid carved Corinthian columns. An extensive Napa Valley wine list and a fine collection of old Ports and Sherrys set the stage for tempting cuisine. Delicacies such as smoked quail with mustard sauce and grapes as an hors d'oeuvre, Chateaubriand for two, and scrumptious chocolate tortes make for a memorable meal.

If you can pull yourself away from La Playa's lush formal gardens and heated swimming pool, there are myriad recreational options in the area, including Pebble Beach, Spy Glass and Carmel Valley Country Club golf courses. The boutique shops and galleries of Carmel village are just 4 blocks from the hotel.

For the meeting-minded, a conference coordinator is on the premises and complete business facilities are available.

THE GOLDEN DOOR

The world's smallest luxury spa resort in the largest Japanese-style building outside Japan, The Golden Door offers coordinated programs to invigorate the body, mind and spirit. Though primarily a women's retreat, it invites couples 6 weeks a year.

The low, graceful complex, patterned after Japan's ancient *honjin* inns, is reached by a 140-foot wooden footbridge. 177 acres of grounds contain a thousand feet of walkways and three courtyards. Each guest room has a wooden ceiling, jalousie windows with *shoji* screens, a traditional *tokonoma* shrine, a private garden view and a moon viewing deck.

Vigorous programs are individually designed for each guest. A typical morning may include a sunrise walk, breakfast in bed, pool exercise, body contouring, steam bath and herbal wrap. The afternoon schedule may include facial and hair treatments, tennis, a twilight walk-jog and meditation. Evening is the time for flower arranging classes, lectures and folk dancing.

The Golden Door's low-calorie gourmet cuisine is world-famous. Most of the produce served by the kitchen is grown on the premises, as are chickens. How Chef Kim Hutchinson creates such natural-food masterpieces as a 300-calorie dinner of tabbouleh salad with fresh cranberries, Chinese stir-fry vegetables with jumbo prawns, and tangerine ice, is a secret he loves to share.

Address: P.O. Box 1567, Escondido 92025; 777 Deer Springs Rd., San Marcos
Phone No.: 619-744-5777
Rates: $$$$
Credit Cards: AmEx, Visa, MC
No. of Rooms: 40
Services and Amenities: Gift shop, Valet service, Library, Limousine airport service, Laundry, Complimentary shoeshine, Complimentary newspaper, Audio cassette player, Radio, Complimentary skin care products, Hair dryer, Makeup lights Beauty shop, Car hire
Restrictions: No pets; no children under 17; no handicapped access
Room Service: 6:00 a.m.-11:00 p.m.
Restaurant: In-house kitchen facility, 7:00-8:00 a.m., 1:00-2:00 p.m., 7:00-8:00 p.m.
Sports Facilities: 2 asphalt tennis courts, full health spa, 2 swimming pools, indoor & outdoor Jacuzzi
Location: Rural area. Guests are requested to remain on premises during their week-long visit

CHATEAU MARMONT

Address: 8221 Sunset Blvd., Hollywood 90046
Phone No.: 213-656-1010
Toll-free Cable: 800-CHATEAU
Telex: TWX 910-321-3006
Rates: $*
Credit Cards: All major credit cards
No. of Rooms: 16 **Suites:** 56
Services and Amenities: Valet service, Garage and parking, Car hire, House doctor, Baby-sitting service, Laundry, Telephone, TV, Radio, Robes
Restrictions: No handicapped access
Room Service: 6:30 a.m.-Midnight
Business Facilities: Copiers, Telex
Sports Facilities: Swimming pool
Location: Sunset Strip, Hollywood
Attractions: Beverly Hills, Rodeo Drive (3 mi.), Hollywood Bowl (3 mi.), Downtown (6 mi.), LAX (10 mi.), Hollywood (2 mi.)

Jean Harlow lived in this hotel's all-white Honeymoon Suite for over a year. The guest register also contains the "autographs" of Hedy Lamar, Humphrey Bogart, Rita Hayworth, Greta Garbo and John Wayne among its many notable guests. Today the newly renovated Chateau Marmont is an Historical-Cultural Monument recalling Hollywood's "Big Studio" era—and its discreet, attentive staff still plays host to the greatest names in filmdom.

Guest accommodations include bright, airy single rooms, bungalows by the year-round heated swimming pool, and many suites. The coveted Penthouse Suite affords perhaps the most glorious city view in all of Los Angeles. Bungalows and suites feature working fireplaces, private backyards and fully-equipped kitchens.

The Chateau Marmont has no restaurant or bar; its clientele seeks privacy, and management has made every attempt to discourage "street traffic." Room service, however, stands ready to serve cheese platters, croissants, caviar and a full menu of other delicacies, as well as fine wines and champagnes from the Chateau's acclaimed cellars.

An oasis of solitude above the glitter of Sunset Boulevard, Chateau Marmont is one of Hollywood's best-kept secrets. Now you know (please don't breathe a word).

HERITAGE HOUSE

Word-of-mouth alone has made this romantic country inn among the most popular on the northern California coast. Total peace reigns, and every part of the grounds affords a spectacular view of the rocky coastline and surrounding forest.

The Heritage House was built in 1877 in the "State of Maine" architectural style popular during that period. The original owners' family still own and operate the inn today. The main building contains some guest rooms, but most accommodations are in cottages nestled throughout the grounds.

The atmosphere is one of informality and relaxation. Here you will find no in-room TVs, or radios, or telephones. Simply one of the most romantic and beautiful spots on the entire Pacific coast, enhanced by gracious service and delicious food.

If you need a break from all this serenity, venture into the nearby historic village of Mendocino. Quaint, charming and quite active, the town offers excellent restaurants, fascinating shops, and galleries displaying works by the many artists who have chosen to call Mendocino their home.

In the spring and fall, guests often sight great gray whales on their migration between the Bering Sea and Mexico.

Address: 5200 North Highway 1, Little River 95456
Phone No.: 707-937-5885
Rates: $$
No. of Rooms: 67 **Suites:** 9
Services and Amenities: Gift shop, soaps
Restrictions: No pets; handicapped access to a few rooms
Restaurant: Dining Room 8:00-10:30 a.m., 6:00-8:30 p.m.
Bar: Applehouse Lounge 3:30 p.m.-Midnight
Location: Rural
Attractions: Local theatre group, shopping in Mendocino, Winetasting Festival, whale watching, old homes tour, art auction

STANFORD PARK HOTEL

Address: 100 El Camino Real, Menlo Park 94025
Phone No.: 415-322-1234
Toll-free Cable: 800-368-2468
Reservation Services: Best Western, 800-528-1234
Rates: $$
Credit Cards: AmEx, Visa, MC, DC, CB
No. of Rooms: 164 **Suites:** 8
Services and Amenities: Valet service, Parking, Car hire, Shuttle to shopping mall, Laundry, Complimentary newspaper, Telephone, Cable TV, Radio, Complimentary toiletries, Dry bar, Phone in bath, Double vanities, Fireplace rooms
Restrictions: No pets; handicapped access to 2 rooms
Room Service: 6:00 a.m.-10:00 p.m.
Restaurant: Palm Cafe, 6:30 a.m.-10:00 p.m.
Bar: Lobby Lounge, 11:00 a.m.-1:30 a.m.
Business Facilities: Message center, Copiers, Audio-visual, Computer hookups
Conference Rooms: 3, capacity 150
Sports Facilities: Health club facilities, Whirlpool, Weights, Sauna, Swimming pool
Location: 45 min. South of San Francisco, 25 min. North of San Jose
Attractions: Stanford Shopping Center, Stanford University, Peninsula wine touring

Newly built in 1984 just minutes from the heart of Silicon Valley and right across the street from the Stanford Shopping Center, this hotel shows a thoughtful blending of yesterday and today. Massive brass doors open into a lobby softly lit by many skylights in the high beamed ceiling. A graceful carved oak staircase and brick fireplace complement the lovely color scheme of burgundy, rose and forest green.

Seventeen different guest room floor plans offer a wide choice to suit your exact needs. Each room has English yew wood furniture custom-designed for the hotel. Each has an executive desk and an armoire with dry bar. The spacious baths and dressing areas glow with the rich sheen of Brazilian granite and tile.

The Palm Cafe is a sunny, cheerful setting for the many grilled entrees and California cuisine specialties. The lobby lounge has suede bar stools and large chairs covered in Pendleton wool; a crackling fire makes this a cozy spot in which to unwind.

The enclosed courtyard contains a heated pool and a large whirlpool bath. There are also a sauna and a physical fitness room equipped with weights.

Special emphasis is on providing every service and convenience for the business traveler. Among the facilities are computer modem hookups. In lieu of room keys, guests open their doors with electronic cards—an appropriate touch considering this hotel's location in the "high-tech" capital of America.

HOTEL BEL-AIR

Address: 701 Stone Canyon Rd., Los Angeles 90077
Phone No.: 213-472-1211
Telex: 674151
Reservation Services: Leading Hotels, Preferred Hotels
Rates: $$$*
Credit Cards: All major credit cards
No. of Rooms: 92 **Suites:** 33
Services and Amenities: Valet service, Car hire, Parking available, Currency exchange, Laundry, Complimentary shoeshine, Baby-sitting service, House doctor on request, Cable TV, Radio, Phone, Robes, Specially packaged complimentary toiletries.
Restrictions: No pets; handicapped access to 2 rooms
Concierge: 24 hours
Room Service: 24 hours
Restaurant: Hotel Bel-Air Restaurant, 7:00-10:30 a.m., 11:30 a.m.-2:00 p.m., 6:00 p.m.-10:30 p.m., Dress Code
Bar: Hotel Bel-Air Bar, 10:00 a.m.-2:00 a.m.
Business Facilities: Services available on request
Sports Facilities: Swimming pool; golf arranged
Location: 45 min. from downtown, 30 min. from airport, 5 min. from major highway
Attractions: 1 mi. from Rodeo Drive, Close to Century City, Westwood and Beverly Hills

Where else can you be surrounded by fountains and courtyards, beside waterfalls that tumble into a lake that hosts a family of white swans—a short drive from Rodeo Drive? Nestled in an eleven-and-a-half-acre estate garden, where redwoods, pampas grass, orchids, lilies and roses blend to create a fabulous color array, The Bel-Air is a most private, secluded and unhurried Shangri La. Accommodations are in mission-style buildings and bungalows. The designers who worked on the project are James Northcutt, Louis Cataffo, Therese Wills, Kalef Alaton and Betty Garber. Each spacious guest room or suite is individually decorated, reflecting the different designers' styles. The atmosphere is opulent, luxurious and quintessentially comfortable. Wood-burning fireplaces, bay windows with window seats, and hand-stencilled ceilings are featured throughout. The lush baths and separate vanity areas gleam with marble and brass fixtures.

The Hotel Bel-Air restaurant is renowned for its California-inspired cuisine. Original art enhances walls upholstered in peachey beige; strikingly beautiful carpeting in a moss green and beige floral pattern unifies the whole. Tables are set with the finest crystal, china and silver.

Our recent dinner experience at the Bel-Air began with California shellfish, crispy sweetbreads and foie gras salad served warm with curly lettuce, walnuts and mint. As an entree, salmon grilled over charcoal with garlic cream, or squab with sweet corn and red pepper relish, is exquisite, as is the pine nut tart with homemade ice cream for dessert. Weather permitting (and it usually is), al fresco dining is available by the pool or on the bougainvillaea draped terrace overlooking the hotel gardens.

The wood-panelled bar has a baby grand piano, fireplace, and fresh flowers. Howard Hughes used the Bel-Air's bar as an informal "office," and the aura of intimacy remains.

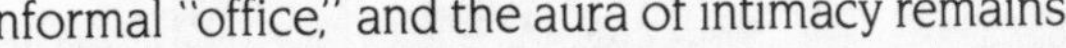

SAN YSIDRO RANCH

A live-and-let-live attitude in the total privacy made possible by 550 acres of wild surrounding foothills explains why the guest list at San Ysidro Ranch is second to none. This charming cottage colony is especially designed as a getaway for lovers of nature, solitude and casual elegance.

The ranch has no "typical" rooms, since no two are alike. Each cottage is individually furnished; all have wood-burning fireplaces and redwood decks with ocean and mountain views, and some have their own Jacuzzis.

The ranch is particularly well-equipped for the sports loving guest. San Ysidro's own stables offer horses for both expert and novice riders, and guided outings are available. There are three tennis courts and a large heated pool. Guests are also extended privileges to the Montecito Country Club's 18-hole golf course.

High beamed ceilings remain from the days when the Plow and Angel Dining Room was a citrus packing house. Now as luxurious as its origins were humble, candlelight dinner here is an extraordinary treat. Chef Wendy Little is renowned throughout California for her exquisite interpretations of classic continental cuisine. A typical dinner might include mussels maison, veal piccata with lemon butter and capers, and Grand Marnier souffle. The wine cellar is outstanding. Before your meal you may wish to stop in at the favorite San Ysidro meeting spot, the Hacienda Lounge.

Address: 900 San Ysidro Lane, Montecito 93108
Phone No.: 805-969-5046
Rates: $$*
Credit Cards: Visa, MC, AmEx
No. of Rooms: 39 **Suites:** 19
Services and Amenities: Valet service, House doctor, Baby-sitting service, Laundry, Complimentary newspaper, Radio, Phone, Robes, Shampoo
Room Service: During meal hours
Restaurant: Plow and Angel Restaurant, 8:00-10:30 a.m., Noon-2:00 p.m., 6:00 p.m. on, Dress Code
Bar: Plow and Angel, 6:00 p.m. on
Business Facilities: Message center, Copiers, Audio-visual
Conference Rooms: 2, capacity 50
Sports Facilities: 3 tennis courts, swimming pool, croquet, riding, hiking, badminton, 2 mi. to 18-hole golf course at Montecito Country Club
Attractions: 5 mi. to Santa Barbara-beaches, Santa Barbara Mission, Courthouse, Art & History Museum, Botanical Gardens

CLAREMONT HOTEL

Claremont Resort Hotel & Tennis Club
Address: P.O. Box 23363, Ashby & Domingo, Oakland 94623
Phone Nos.: 843-3000; Reservations 843-7924
Rates: $$*
Credit Cards: Visa, MC, CB, DC, AmEx
No. of Rooms: 236 **Suites:** 16
Services and Amenities: Gift shop, Valet Service, Barber shop, Parking, Car hire, Baby-sitting service, Laundry, Complimentary newspaper, TV, Radio, Phone, Bidet, Sun lamps, Soap, Shampoo, Vitabath
Concierge: 9:00 a.m.-6:00 p.m.
Room Service: 6:30 a.m.-10:00 p.m.
Restaurant: Pavilion Room, 6:30-11:00 a.m., 11:30 a.m.-2:00 p.m., 6:00-10:00 p.m., Dress Code; Presto Cafe
Bar: Terrace Bar, 11:30 a.m.-2:00 a.m.
Business Facilities: Front desk message center, Copiers, Audio-visual
Conference Rooms: 22
Sports Facilities: 10 tennis courts, Swimming Pool, Par course, Ping-pong, Whirlpool, Sauna, Massage, Aerobics
Attractions: Tours of wine country, San Francisco Bay boat excursions, University of California Botanical Garden and Tilden Recreation Area close by

The Claremont is the only major resort in the central San Francisco Bay area. Situated on 22 exquisitely landscaped acres in the Oakland-Berkeley hills, this 1915 Victorian landmark has been maintained in grand style.

The gardens, filled with cutting-edge art, are riotously in bloom the greater part of the year. The public areas, done in a lovely peach hue, display an extensive collection of sculpture and paintings. The rooms are large and comfortable, and many have exquisite bay views.

The Pavilion Room restaurant has an elegant, ethereal atmosphere that captures the stunning bay vista and magnifies it with gleaming silver and a wall of mirrors. The cuisine is contemporary California with a classic French accent. There is an *a la carte* menu as well as a daily *prix fixe* menu.

Our dinner began with a rich mussel and watercress soup, followed by a raddichio and mushroom salad. One entree was a broiled rib eye steak with a bourbon and mustard beurre blanc.

Another was roast breast of veal stuffed with pistacchios and spinach. Both were accompanied by baby vegetables, sourdough bread and butter rosettes. Dessert was a choice of gateau, tarts, or cheese and fruit. As a final fillip, we were served long-stemmed strawberries dipped in bittersweet chocolate. The wine list was extensive, and there was a fully-stocked cordial cart.

Recreational facilities at the Claremont include ten asphalt tennis courts and a spectacular Olympic-size swimming pool.

There are full conference facilities for business meetings. The central location provides easy access to San Francisco and the South Bay, as well as the booming Berkeley and Oakland business areas.

MAXIM'S DE PARIS

Pierre Cardin-designed Parisian elegance in the middle of the California desert? When international hotel and casino entrepreneur Jack Pratt acquired U.S. rights to the prestigeous Maxim's name and announced plans to build the ultimate resort in southern California's legendary golf mecca, some onlookers were skeptical. But upon the unveiling of this full-service all-suite hotel, all doubts vanished.

Located in the very center of Palm Springs, the project was supervised in every detail by its creator, Pierre Cardin. The ultra-modern architecture by H. K. Smith features a six-story atrium lobby with glass skylight. Fine polished marble and soft muted colors provide an ambience of casual elegance.

The spacious suites contain custom-designed furniture and lush fabrics.Each bathroom is done in imported marble and lavished with fresh flowers. All suites have private balconies commanding impressive views of either Mt. San Jacinto or downtown Palm Springs.

Le Jardin is fashioned after the France's most famous restaurant, Maxim's de Paris. Tables are set with Boscher china, cut crystal and sterling silver. The cuisine, though similar to that of the hotel's European namesake, boasts a unique California Nouvelle flair. A recent dinner of coquille St. Jacques, beef premiere and choice of pastries would rival any feast to be found on either continent.

The Palm Court Lounge, adjoining the magnificent lobby, entertains with piano and harp music. There is also a private pool-side cocktail lounge for that authentic Palm Springs "posh" feeling.

Full conference facilities make Maxim's the ideal setting for business as well as pleasure.

Address: 285 No. Palm Canyon Dr., Palm Springs 92262
Phone No.: 619-322-9000
Toll-free Cable: US 800-5-MAXIMS, CA 800-533-3556
Reservation Services: LRI, 800-223-0888
Rates: $$$*
Credit Cards: AmEx, Visa, MC, CB, DC
No. of Suites: 194
Services and Amenities: Valet service, Barber, Beauty shop, Laundry, Car hire, Currency exchange, Complimentary shoeshine, House doctor, Baby-sitting service, Complimentary newspaper, Cable TV, Radio, Phone, Robes, Whirlpool, Bidet, Sun lamp
Restrictions: No pets; handicapped access to 7 rooms
Concierge: 24 hours
Room Service: 24 hours
Restaurant: Le Jardin, 11:00 a.m.-11:00 p.m., Dress Code
Bar: Palm Court Lounge, 11:00 a.m.-Midnight
Business Facilities: Message center, Secretarial service, Translators, Copiers, Audio-visual, Teleconference, Telex
Conference Rooms: 5, capacity 150
Sports Facilities: Palm Springs Tennis Club; Golf, riding arranged; full health spa, swimming pool
Location: 2 mi. from airport. State Highway 111 to I-10, 10 mi.
Attractions: Aerial Tramway, Desert Fashion Plaza, Desert Museum

INN AT RANCHO SANTA FE

Address: P.O. Box 869, Rancho Santa Fe 92067
Phone Nos: 619-756-1131
Rates: $
Credit Cards All major credit cards
No. of Rooms: 75 **Suites:** 8
Services and Amenities: Valet service, Parking, Car hire, House doctor, Baby-sitting service, Laundry, Game area, TV
Restrictions: Dogs only (extra charge); handicapped access to 2 rooms
Room Service: During meal hours
Restaurant: Garden Room and Vintage Room, 7:00-10:30 a.m., Noon-2:30 p.m., 6:30-9:00 p.m., Dress Code
Bar: Vintage Room, 11:00 a.m.-11:00 p.m.
Business Facilities: Message center, Translators, Copiers, Audio-visual
Conference Rooms: 2, capacity 25-100
Sports Facilities: 3 hard-surface tennis courts, croquet, 18-hole golf course, riding, swimming pool
Attractions: Sea World, San Diego Zoo, Wild Animal Park, Museum in La Jolla

The Inn at Rancho Santa Fe, 25 miles from San Diego, is one of those discreet spots to which a loyal and devoted clientele returns year after year. Amid towering eucalyptus and citrus groves, the inn offers pure serenity.

Most accommodations are in cottages scattered about the property. Each cottage room has been individually decorated, and nearly all have secluded porches or sun decks. Rooms with fireplaces and kitchens, and interconnecting suites for larger groups, are available.

The inn offers fine dining in a variety of settings. The Library is filled with books and firelight. The Vintage Room, a replica of an early California taproom, opens onto a patio where guests dine under the stars on summer weekend evenings. The Garden Room, all lattices and flowers, affords a sweeping view across the inn's emerald lawns and pool. The cuisine is fine classic American.

The 20-acre beautifully landscaped grounds bloom almost continuously. Guests enjoy not only the inn's heated pool and three tennis courts, but also privileges at the famous Rancho Santa Fe Club. For ocean swimming, the inn has a beach cottage with showering and dressing facilities at nearby Del Mar Beach. Within an hour's drive are San Diego's Zoo and Sea World, the old gold mining town of Julian, and perhaps a quick step across the border into colorful Mexico.

CAMPTON PLACE

Address: 340 Stockton St., San Francisco 94108
Phone No.: 415-781-5555
Toll-free Cable: 800-647-4007 US, 800-235-4300 CA
Telex: 6771185 CPTN
Reservation Services: LRI, 800-223-0888
Rates: $$$*
Credit Cards: MC, Visa, AmEx, CB, DC
No. of Rooms: 126
Suites: 10
Services and Amenities: Valet service, Parking, International currency exchange, Laundry, Complimentary shoeshine, House doctor, Baby-sitting service, Bath phone, Amenities from I. Magnin, Terry towels and robes
Restrictions: Small pets; handicapped access to 3 rooms
Concierge: 24 hours
Room Service: 7:00 a.m.-11:00 p.m.
Restaurant: Campton Place Restaurant, 7:00 a.m.-10:30 p.m. daily, Dress Code
Bar: Campton, 7:00 a.m.-11:00 p.m.
Business Facilities: Message center, Secretarial service, Copiers, Telex, Word processing available
Conference Rooms: 2, capacity 10 and 14
Location: Union Square
Attractions: Maiden Lane boutique shopping, Union Square major shopping district, near cable car line

The exterior is Spanish revival, the interior contemporary, and the location the best: one-half block from Union Square, and only 4 blocks from San Francisco's financial district. Opened in 1983, Campton Place is the proud result of an $18 million total renovation of two turn-of-the-century buildings.

The peach-and-taupe color scheme used throughout complements exquisite furnishings and distinctive objets d'art. The 126 rooms and suites are residential in character and quite luxurious.

Armoires conceal remote control color TV. Beds are made up with the softest sheets, down comforters and down pillows. Bathrooms are of travertine marble with brass fixtures. Other amenities include a wall telephone in the bathroom, a full complement of I. Magnin toiletries and a bathrobe. The service is professional, friendly and prompt.

Campton Place restaurant has emerged during the past few years as one of the state's leading restaurants. The dining room decor shines with Wedgwood china, fine linen, crystal, and oriental porcelains, but the food itself upstages all else.

Chef Bradley Ogden is a culinary master. Don't miss breakfast, whether poached eggs and Missouri ham on oven-hot biscuits with orange hollandaise, or a warm spiced compote of nectarines, blueberries, bananas, papaya and apples. Lunch and dinner specialties include wild mushrooms in cream and sherry with herb crust, grilled quail with smoked bacon, limestone lettuce with triple cream blue cheese, and a flourless chocolate cake for dessert.

Everything on the restaurant menu (which changes regularly) is also available via room service for *en suite* dining privacy.

THE HUNTINGTON

The height of elegance in San Francisco is to be found atop Nob Hill in the classic and understated Huntington. Built as a residence hotel in 1924 by the architectural firm of Weeks and Day, the Huntington is now the pride of the Cope family, innkeepers extraordinaire.

You will sense the atmosphere of quiet luxury and security as the doorman admits you to the intimate lobby, and you will understand why visiting nobility and celebrities of opera, symphony and stage choose The Huntington.

The stylish, comfortable rooms, each different, have been designed by Anthony Hail, Lee Radziwill and Elizabeth Bernhardt. All are spacious and elegantly furnished. Of the 30 suites, our personal favorite is the Ambassador Suite (#1207), with its ornate gilt ceiling and 17th- and 18th-Century Italian furnishings. Robert Redford slept here; so did Baron Edmond de Rothschild. Luciano Pavarotti's choice, Suite #514, is done in delightful yellow and aqua English chintz with a Chinese motif. Each suite has both kitchen and separate dining room, and the bedroom is set peacefully away from the living area.

The Big Four Restaurant and Bar, named for the Central Pacific railroad magnates, offers continental and American cuisine in a refined atmosphere of green leather banquettes and rich gleaming mahogany. We recommend the Boule de Niege for dessert. The cozy bar is a San Francisco favorite. The Huntington also boasts the world-renowned French restaurant, L'Etoile.

Address: 1075 California Street, San Francisco 94108
Phone No.: 415-474-5400
Toll-free Cable: 800-227-4683 US, 800-652-1539 CA
Telex: 857363
Reservation Services: Small Luxury Hotels, 800-862-7272, or Distinguished Hotels, 800-792-7637
Rates: $$*
Credit Cards: AmEx, Visa, MC, DC, CB
No. of Rooms: 100 **Suites:** 43
Services and Amenities: Valet service, Garage & parking, Chauffeured limo, Laundry, House doctor, Radio, Complimentary newspaper, Cable TV, Shampoo, Soap, Shoeshine cloth, Bath gel, Hairdryers
Restrictions: No pets
Concierge: 7:00 a.m.-11:00 p.m.
Room Service: 7:00 a.m.-10:00 p.m.
Restaurant: The Big Four, 7:00-9:30 a.m., 11:30 a.m.-3:00 p.m., 5:30-11:00 p.m.; Sat.-Sun. brunch 9:00 a.m. -3:00 p.m.
Bar: The Big Four, 11:30 a.m.-1:00 a.m.
Business Facilities: Message center, Secretarial service, Translators, Copiers, Audio-visual, Telex
Conference Rooms: 1, capacity 40
Location: Nob Hill
Attractions: On cable car line

THE DONATELLO

Address: 501 Post St., San Francisco 94102
Phone No.: 415-441-7100
Telex: 172875
Rates: $$$*
Credit Cards: AmEx, Visa, MC, DC, JCB
No. of Rooms: 95 **Suites:** 5
Services and Amenities: Valet service, Laundry, Garage and parking, Car hire, Complimentary shoeshine, House doctor, Babysitting service, Complimentary newspaper, TV, Radio, Bath phone, Robes, Gucci perfumes, Fine soaps
Restrictions: No pets; no handicapped access
Concierge: 9:00 a.m.-6:00 p.m.
Room Service: 6:00 a.m.-Midnight
Restaurant: Ristorante Donatello, 7:00-10:30 a.m., 11:30 a.m.-2:30 p.m., 6:00-10:30 p.m., Dress Code
Bar: In restaurant, 11:30 a.m.-1:00 a.m.
Business Facilities: Secretarial service, Translators, Copiers, Audio-visual, Telex
Conference Rooms: 2, capacity 65
Sports Facilities: Full health spa, Whirlpool, Sauna, Access to outside health clubs booked through concierge
Location: Union Square
Attractions: Boutique shopping, Major theatre district

"Italian design, craftsmanship, cuisine and staff are perfectly integrated at the Donatello," says A. Cal Rossi Jr., the creative force behind this remarkable hotel in the heart of San Francisco's fashionable shopping and theatre district. The Italian sculptor Donatello was a major figure in 15th-Century Renaissance art, and the hotel bearing his name reflects classic European spirit.

The interiors, designed by Andrew Delfino, blend travertine, Italian marble, Venetian glass and European antiques. The spacious guest rooms are luxuriously decorated in soft pastels and designer prints, with Ming and Biedermeier furnishings. In the marble-clad baths you will find Gucci perfumes and full-length terry cloth robes. Our favorite suite has a bedroom done in cream color with dark details, with a fine corner view. The living room has walls covered in Fortuny fabrics, couches in pale rose, and an impressive marble entryway.

Ristorante Donatello has been an international success since the day it opened. Its two dining rooms are done in Fortuny fabrics with Veronese marble floors. The atmosphere, while elegant and formal, maintains an intimate ambience and charm.

A springtime dinner opened with a creamy risotto with truffles and wild mushrooms, followed by fresh monkfish sauteed with two pepper sauces, accompanied by Favorita di Santa Vittoria d'Alba. The next course was medallions of veal sauteed with fresh sage and butter. Dessert was dark chocolate fondant in a light orange-scented custard, delicious with Moscato Rosa. The feast would have impressed even the Medici. Besides daily special dinners such as this, there is an extensive a la carte menu.

Sophisticated travelers from the U.S. and abroad have fallen in love with *il dolce far niete* at the Donatello. You will too.

THE INN AT THE OPERA

This 48-room luxury hotel is located in the heart of the performing arts center, just steps from the opera, symphony and Museum of Modern Art. The ideal home-away-from-home for lovers of the arts, it is also convenient to shopping, fine restaurants and downtown business offices.

Each guest room is done in a soft pastel palette and filled with custom-made furnishings. Beds are lavishly provided with oversized pillows, and a plush terry robe hangs in the armoire for your use. The lovely baths, in classic European white-on-white decor, have telephone and TV for your convenience, as well as a basket filled with luxury toiletries just for fun. A representative suite has a large sitting area in a soft peaches-and-cream color scheme, complete with wet bar. The cozy bedroom has its own sitting area and a full bath. The average suite size is 400 square feet.

The Inn at the Opera is fortunate to have the wonderful Act IV Lounge, a favorite meeting place for performing artists and patrons. This sumptuous room reminds one of a blue velvet jewel box. Breakfast, lunch, dinner and apres-theatre are served daily until 1:00 a.m. The innovative menu emphasizes light, fresh bistro cuisine. After the theatre, you may enjoy Giverney salad of greens, blossoms and fresh herbs with a hazelnut vinaigrette, or perhaps you would prefer spanakopita spinach and feta cheese wrapped in filo, or steak tartare. Enjoy the warmth of the fireplace while listening to romantic, classical and jazz music played on the grand piano.

The complimentary bottle of chilled white wine in your room should get your visit off to a fine start.

Address: 333 Fulton Street, San Francisco 94102
Phone No.: 415-863-8400
Toll-free Cable: 800-325-2708 US, 800-423-9610 CA
Rates: $$
Credit Cards: MC, Visa, DC, AmEx, CB
No. of Rooms: 48
Suites: 12
Services and Amenities: Laundry, Valet service, House doctor, Complimentary newspaper, TV, Radio, Telephone, Robes, Basket of bath amenities
Restrictions: No pets; handicapped access to 6 rooms
Room Service: 6:30 a.m.-2:30 a.m.
Restaurant: Act IV, 6:30 a.m.-2:00 a.m.
Bar: Same as restaurant
Business Facilities: Message center, Copiers, Secretarial service and audio-visual available
Conference Rooms: 1, capacity 12
Location: Civic and Performing Arts Center
Attractions: Opera, Ballet, Symphony, Museum

HOTEL DIVA

Address: 440 Geary St., San Francisco 94102
Phone No.: 415-885-0200
Toll-free Cable: 800-553-1900
Telex: 470429
Reservation Services: VIP/HSI
Rates: $$*
Credit Cards: All major credit cards including JCB
No. of Rooms: 124 **Suites:** 30 mini-suites
Services and Amenities: Valet service, Library, Garage and parking, Car hire, Laundry, Complimentary shoeshine, House doctor, Baby-sitting service, Card area, Complimentary newspaper, TV, Radio, Video cassette player, Sun lamp, Imported soaps, bath gels and shampoos
Restrictions: No pets; handicapped access to 1 room on each of 6 floors
Concierge: 7:00 a.m.-11:00 p.m.
Room Service: 7:00 a.m.-Midnight
Restaurant: 11:00 a.m.-1:00 a.m., Dress Code
Business Facilities: Message center, Secretarial service, Translators, Copiers, Audio-visual, Teleconferencing, Telex, Complete business center
Conference Rooms: 3, capacity 15-20
Location: Union Square
Attractions: Boutiques on Maiden Lane, Union Square shopping, Theatres

The renaissance/baroque-style exterior remains as originally constructed in 1912, but the bold Italian avante garde interior, with its gleaming steel and plush leather club chairs, is all new.
The spacious guest rooms in bold colors contain imported furnishings such as the famous Tizio lamps. Curl up in bed under a delightful down comforter to enjoy movies on the VCR. "High-tech" designer bathrooms feature marble fixtures and bright white tile, with stainless steel sinks for contrast. Even the bath amenities are custom designed. The Villa Suite, with its shiny white lacquer, arched windows, deluxe leather lounge chairs and marble dining table, shows how exciting hotel room decor can be. The classic Italian restaurant fits right in. Every detail of the Hotel Diva bespeaks continental style as progressive as tomorrow.

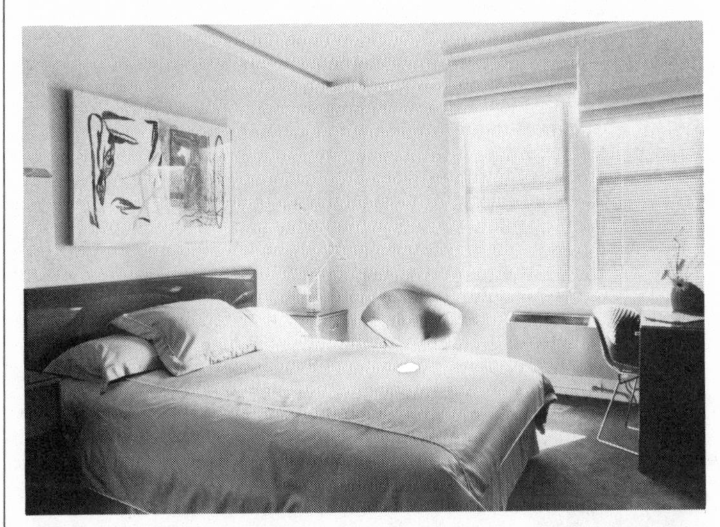

YORK HOTEL

The dream to be pampered lives in all of us, and this affordably elegant hotel is designed for dreams to come true—executive gym, conference room, limousine service, a cabaret featuring famous-name entertainment, and complimentary continental breakfast served in your room by a conscientious, attentive staff member.

Just four blocks from Union Square on lower Nob Hill, the hotel is surrounded by San Francisco's best boutiques, galleries, restaurants, cafes and theatres.

All the original 1922 architectural features have been retained in the hotel's renovation, and you may recognize it as the location for a key scene between James Stewart and Kim Novak in Hitchcock's *Vertigo*, filmed here in 1955. The grandeur of earlier times is complemented today with contemporary furnishings in a soft pastel colors.

The intimate, richly decorated Plush Room, with its lustrous rosewood bar and fabulous stained-glass ceiling, showcases jazz, contemporary music and the latest cabaret shows.

Address: 940 Sutter St., San Francisco 94109
Phone No.: 415-885-6800
Toll-free: 800-227-3608 US, 800-327-3608 CA
Reservation Services: VIP 415-969-1232
Rates: $
Credit Cards: AmEx, MC, Visa, DC, CB
No. of Rooms: 94 **Suites:** 5
Services and Amenities: Laundry, Valet service, Garage and parking, Baby-sitting service, Complimentary newspaper, Cable TV, Shampoo, Conditioner, Sewing Kit, Shoeshine, Glycerine soap
Restrictions: No pets; no handicapped access
Concierge: Wed.-Sun. 9:00 a.m.-5:00 p.m.
Room Service: 7:00 a.m.-11:00 p.m.
Bar: Plush Room, 5:00 p.m.-1:00 a.m.
Business Facilities: Copiers, Telex, Access to secretarial service, Audio-visual equipment upon request
Conference Rooms: 2, capacity 160
Location: Downtown

HOTEL VINTAGE COURT

Address: 650 Bush St., San Francisco 94108
Phone No.: 415-392-4666
Toll-free Cable: US 800-654-1100, CA 800-654-7266
Rates: $
Credit Cards: MC, AmEx
No. of Rooms: 106
Services and Amenities: Valet service, Car hire, House doctor, Complimentary wine 4:00-6:00 p.m., Laundry, Wet bar, Baby-sitting service, Phones, TV
Restrictions: Seeing Eye dogs permitted; handicapped access to 7 rooms
Concierge: 24 hours
Restaurant: Masa's, Tue.-Sat. 6:00-11:00 p.m., by reservation only, 21 days in advance
Bar: Masa's, Tue.-Sat. 6:00-11:00 p.m.
Business Facilities: Message center, Secretarial service, Copiers, Audio-visual, Telex
Conference Rooms: 1, capacity 15
Sports Facilities: Access to Health Club
Location: 1½ blocks from Union Square, 10 blocks from highway, 20 miles from airport

Vintage California wines are this hotel's theme: a cellar filled with boutique wines, complimentary fireside wine-tasting, tours of the wine country by custom Rolls Royce, horse-drawn carriage or hot-air balloon.

The hotel, built in 1912, was completely restored in 1983. Its 106 guest rooms, named after vineyards, are decorated in soothing pastel Laura Ashley prints and fabrics. Each large room is provided with ample amenities including a wet bar.

Wine-tasting is held from 4:00 to 6:00 p.m. daily in the elegant sitting room off the lobby. Guests seem to have a wonderful time relaxing in overstuffed chairs beside the crackling fire.

Masa's is ranked among the nation's finest French restaurants. Enjoy specialties like sauteed foie gras with truffles, roast pheasant layered with fresh pear, and fine pastries (and rare vintage wines, of course). The restaurant has only twelve tables; call at least three weeks in advance to make your dinner reservation!

The hotel is just one-and-a-half blocks from Union Square shopping, galleries, boutiques. Guests are extended privileges to the Nob Hill Health Club.

All this, at a surprisingly reasonable cost, explains why the Hotel Vintage Court has one of the highest occupancy rates in San Francisco.

THE ORCHARD HOTEL

Next door to the Yves St. Laurent Rive Gauche Boutique, within minutes' walk of the cable car to Fisherman's Wharf, and four blocks from Chinatown, The Orchard feels truly international. The lobby is a charming little jewel box in shades of rose and pale green damask with a glittering crystal chandelier and a grand piano. Its floor-to-ceiling windows look out onto fashionable Sutter Street.

Rooms are traditionally furnished with custom-made European furniture, including fully stocked mahogany minibars, to create a comfortable home-away-from-home atmosphere. The baths have international direct-dial telephones and ample personal care amenities.

Adjacent to the lobby's lounge bar is the fashionable Annabel Restaurant, a favorite San Francisco "in spot" thanks to its remarkable nouvelle cuisine, splendid decor and exceptional service.

Address: 562 Sutter Street, San Francisco 94102
Phone No.: 415-433-4434
Telex: 171500
Rates: $
Credit Cards: AmEx, CB, DC, Visa, MC
No. of Rooms: 96 **Suites:** 2
Services and Amenities: Laundry, Valet service, Car hire, Babysitting service, Complimentary newspaper, TV with clock, Radio, Mini-bar fully stocked, Telephone, Bidet, Shampoo, Hand lotion, Bath gel
Restrictions: No pets; handicapped access to 6 rooms
Concierge: 7:00 a.m.-10:00 p.m.
Room Service: 7:00 a.m.-10:00 p.m.
Restaurant: Annabel's, 7:00 a.m.-10:00 p.m., Dress Code
Bar: 11:00 a.m.-10:00 p.m.
Business Facilities: Copiers, Telex
Conference Rooms: 1, capacity 14
Location: Union Square
Attractions: Shopping, Art galleries

THE SAINTE CLAIRE

The Sainte Claire Hilton
Address: 302 South Market St., San Jose 95113
Phone No.: 408-295-2000
Telex: 176880
Reservation Services: HRS 800-HILTONS
Rates: $*
Credit Cards: Visa, MC, CB, DC, AmEx
No. of Rooms: 184 **Suites:** 13
Services and Amenities: Gift and flower shop, Laundry, Garage and parking, Baby-sitting service, Cable TV, Radio, Telephone, Whirlpool bath, Hilton amenities
Restrictions: No pets; handicapped access to 1 room
Room Service: 6:30 a.m.-10:00 p.m.
Restaurant: T. S. Montgomery, 6:30 a.m.-10:00 p.m., Dress Code; Hamasushi, 11:30 a.m.-11:00 p.m.
Bar: Barrington's, 3:30 p.m.-1:30 a.m.
Business Facilities: Message center, Secretarial service, Copiers, Audio-visual, Telex
Conference Rooms: 10, capacity 10 to 700
Sports Facilities: Park Center Athletic Club 3 min. away; Whirlpool, Sauna
Location: Downtown, 1½ miles or 8 min. from airport, 3 blocks from major highway
Attractions: Near Center for the Performing Arts, Museum of Art, Convention Center, Egyptian Museum

To those who have not visited the Sainte Claire, our listing Silicon Valley's Hilton among America's finest intimate, continental-style hotels may raise a few eyebrows. This, however, is no run-of-the-mill business travelers' hotel; rather, it is the Hilton chain's magnificent historical restoration showpiece. Completely renovated in 1982, this 1920s landmark hotel exudes genuine elegance.

Public rooms have panelled walls more than 20 feet high, illuminated by a collection of priceless crystal chandeliers. The guest room color scheme is serene green, white and peach. The bathrooms retain their fine original porcelain fixtures and large deep bathtubs alongside newly added telephones, TVs, whirlpools and a full complement of quality toiletries. A grand three-room suite will comfortably accommodate 40 people for a cocktail reception.

A recent deluxe dinner in the T. S. Montgomery restaurant featured Shrimp Scampi, Caesar salad for two, and Coquille St. Jacques. Desserts were selected from a French pastry cart. Hamasushi, open for lunch and dinner, offers an array of Japanese delights. Barrington's bar, a favorite local meeting place, has a dance floor and live entertainment.

Ten conference rooms that will hold up to 700 people, and its proximity to Silicon Valley and the Center for the Performing Arts, make the Sainte Claire Hilton a fine stopping place for executive travelers as well as other patrons with a taste for elegance.

EL ENCANTO HOTEL

First built as college residence halls, El Encanto was converted in the early 1900s into a winter cottage resort for the "carriage trade." Today, guests are more likely to arrive in Cadillacs or Jaguars, but the splendor of that bygone era lingers.

El Encanto Hotel and Garden Villas is a classic ten acre resort, with 100 guest rooms and villas nestled in beautifully landscaped gardens, all overlooking Santa Barbara and the ocean. The emphasis is on serenity in fabulous surroundings. The decor is country French, lavish with warm colors and floral prints. No two rooms are identical.

The pool terrace perches like a fragment of the French Riviera above the Pacific coastline, surrounded by banana plants.

The intimate dining terrace is a most romantic rendezvous. The extraordinary wine list, featuring both California and European wines, enhances the pleasures of the gourmet cuisine. A sample of the chef's dishes: angel hair pasta with lobster, medallions of veal, port wine sauce and artichoke mousse, and a sumptuous floating island for dessert.

El Encanto is fully equipped to handle conferences for from 60 to 140 persons. State-of-the-art audio-visual and communications technology is available.

El Encanto Hotel & Garden Villas
Address: 1900 Lasuen Road, Santa Barbara 93103
Phone No.: 805-687-5000
Telex: 658304
Rates: $$$
Credit Cards: AmEx, Visa, MC
No. of Rooms: 100 **Suites:** 75
Services and Amenities: Laundry, Valet service, Parking, Car hire, Baby-sitting service, Complimentary newspaper, Cable TV, Telephone, Robes, Standard amenity package
Restrictions: No pets; no handicapped access
Concierge: 8:00 a.m.-10:00 p.m.
Room Service: 6:30 a.m.-9:00 p.m.
Restaurant: El Encanto Dining Room, 7:00 a.m.-10:00 p.m.
Bar: El Encanto Lounge, 11:00 a.m.-Midnight
Business Facilities: Message center, Copiers, Audio-visual, Telex
Conference Rooms: 6, capacity 140
Sports Facilities: Tennis court, swimming pool, access to Montecito Country Club, riding, polo, sailing
Location: Riviera section in hills overlooking Santa Barbara
Attractions: Walking distance to historic Santa Barbara Mission, 5 min. to downtown and beach

THE WOODMARK

Address: 5415 Stevens Creek Blvd., Santa Clara 95051
Phone No.: 408-446-3030
Rates: $$
Credit Cards: All major credit cards
No. of Rooms: 60 **Suites:** 8
Services and Amenities: Laundry, Valet service, Library, Parking, Car hire, Baby-sitting service, Complimentary newspaper, TV, VCR, Telephone, Robes, Complimentary toiletries, Sachet, Shoe sponge, Shower cap, Sewing kit
Restrictions: No pets; handicapped access to 3 rooms
Restaurant: Private dining room for guests, 5:00 p.m.-Midnight
Bar: In dining room
Business Facilities: Message center, Secretarial service, Copiers, Audio-visual, Access to complete business center and private carrier service
Conference Rooms: 3, capacity 6-12
Location: Silicon Valley
Attractions: Minutes from Vallco Fashion Park and Vallco Village, 5 min. from Flint Center for the Performing Arts, 15 min. from Paul Masson Winery, Ridge and Sunrise Wineries in Montebello foothills

The Woodmark, opened in July 1985, is ready to substantiate its claim of being "as uncommon as our guests." Among the uncommon features are exceptionally attentive personal service, state-of-the-art technology and an environment modeled after a French country estate. The walled perimeter and landscaped atrium courtyard provide a peaceful haven in the very heart of Silicon Valley, just ten minutes from downtown San Jose and fifteen minutes from the airport.

The distinctive decor blends tones of soft rose, gray and pale blue with French country furnishings. Guest rooms feature large work areas with personal computer hook-up capabilities, and cable TVs equipped with VCR units. The hotel has a large video library of feature films as well as blank tape for personal recording. The library also offers top-ten bestsellers and a great variety of magazines.

The bathrooms have vanity-top TVs, telephones, full-length terry robes, and a bountiful selection of personal care amenities.

The Woodmark serves a full complimentary buffet breakfast in the private salon each morning from 6:30 to 10:00 a.m. Guests who choose not to dine at one of the fine restaurants nearby are invited to raid the Woodmark's pantry, always stocked with fruit, sandwiches, hot entrees, ice cream and more. The executive lounge features cocktails and fine California wines.

The Woodmark's meeting rooms accommodate small conferences from 4 to 50 people, and the lovely garden courtyard hosts receptions for up to 100.

SONOMA MISSION INN

Address: 18149 Sonoma Hwy 12, Boyes Hot Springs, P.O. Box 1447, Sonoma 95476
Phone No.: 707-938-9000
Toll-free Cable: CA 800-862-4945, US 800-358-9022
Rates: $$$*
Credit Cards: AmEx, MC, Visa, CB, DC
No. of Rooms: 170 **Suites:** 3
Services and Amenities: Big 3 gourmet market, Valet service, Laundry, Barber shop, Beauty shop, Parking, Car hire, House doctor, Baby-sitting service, Game area, Phone, Cable TV, Radio, Robes, Shampoo, Conditioner, Bath Gel, Salts, Loofah
Restrictions: No pets; adults only in spa; handicapped access to 5 rooms
Concierge: Saturdays
Room Service: 8:00-10:30 a.m.
Restaurant: The Grille, 7:30 a.m.-10:30 p.m.
Bar: The Bar, 11:30 a.m.-2:00 a.m.
Business Facilities: Message center, Copiers, Audio-visual
Conference Rooms: 9, capacity 600
Sports Facilities: 2 hard-surface tennis courts, Bicycling, Hiking, Hot-air balooning, Full health spa, Swimming pool
Location: Boyes Hot Springs
Attractions: Historic town of Sonoma, Shopping for food specialties, General Vallejo's home, Mission San Francisco Solano de Sonoma, Wine tasting

Boyes Hot Springs has been a popular spa resort for over a century. The present inn, built on the site in 1927, was hailed as an architectural *tour de force*—a replicate California mission complete with arcade and bell tower. Since its renovation in 1980, the inn surpasses even its original grandeur.

The inn is located on 8 landscaped acres just outside the town of Sonoma. The interior features shades of pink and gray, and fresh flowers everywhere contribute to the atmosphere of country elegance.

The beds are canopied and the windows are fitted with plantation shutters. Ceiling fans, spacious walk-in closets, and subtle taupe, clay and camel hues create a mellow ambience. The baths are provided with robes and plentiful bath-time treats.

Whether you are slimming deliciously on the spa plan or indulging in The Grille's gourmet fare, the cuisine is extraordinary. Dinner might begin with smoked duck and salmon, followed by a mixed mesquite grill of quail, lamb and Sonoma sausage, accompanied by a fine Sonoma wine (the wine list includes over 200 selections) and completed with Chocolate Decadence.

The Big Three Fountain, a fifties-style soda fountain, is a Sonoma County favorite.

The historic town of Sonoma with its picturesque plaza and fabulous shopping area is nearby, as are the Mission San Francisco Solano de Sonoma and General Vallejo's home.

Enjoy the beautifying rigors of the complete European style fitness program, or simply laze by the pool; the magic of the Sonoma Mission Inn will captivate you.

BEL AGE

The name Bel Age conjures images of a bygone era of leisurely opulence totally appropriate to this world-class all-suite hotel. Located in the fashionable Sunset Plaza district, it lies just minutes from the heart of Beverly Hills and Century City.

Suites are filled with European furniture hand-carved in rosewood and pecan; luxurious fabrics and original art work enhance the mood of comfortable elegance. Each suite also has a wet bar, kitchenette, and three telephones with conferencing capabilities. Bathrooms have TV, telephone, terry cloth robes and lavish personal care amenities.

The lush, landscaped rooftop garden provides an oasis for sunbathing, swimming or enjoying the whirlpool spa and health club facilities.

Two restaurants offer different varieties of fine cuisine. The Bel Age restaurant, with its image of old-world elegance, is an intimate gourmet dining experience. La Brasserie provides an informal bistro atmosphere in the best French tradition. The bar adjoining The Bel Age restaurant is a delightful spot in which to unwind to the strains of piano music.

Special emphasis has been placed on providing every facility for meetings and conferences. Soundproofed board and meeting rooms have the most advanced audio-visual equipment. An expert multilingual staff is on hand to assist.

Address: 1020 N. San Vicente Blvd., West Hollywood 90069
Phone No.: 213-854-1111, 800-424-4443
Telex: 887487 Le Bel Age
Rates: $$$*
Credit Cards: AmEx, Visa, MC, DC
No. of Suites: 198
Services and Amenities: Gift shop, Valet service, Barber shop, Beauty shop, Garage and parking, Car hire, Laundry, Complimentary shoeshine, House doctor, Babysitting service on call, Audio & video cassette players on request, Complimentary newspaper, Cable TV, Radio, Telephone, Robes, Custom-milled soaps, Cologne, Sewing kit, Shower caps
Restrictions: No pets; handicapped access to 2 rooms
Concierge: 7:00 a.m.-6:00 p.m.
Room Service: 24 hours
Restaurant: Bel Age, 6:00 p.m.-11:30 p.m., La Brasserie, 7:00 a.m.-Midnight
Bar: The Bar, 2:00 p.m.-Midnight; La Brasserie Bar, 11:00 a.m.-Midnight
Business Facilities: Message center, Secretarial service on call, Copiers, Audio-visual on request, Telex
Conference Rooms: Grand Ballroom, 2 Grand Salons, 3 meeting rooms
Sports Facilities: Heated swimming pool, whirlpool
Location: West Hollywood

MONDRIAN

Address: 8440 Sunset Boulevard, West Hollywood 90069
Phone No.: 213-650-8999
Telex: 182570 Le Mondrian USA
Reservation Services: 800-424-4443
Rates: $$*
Credit Cards: AmEx, Visa, MC, DC, CB
Suites: 188
Services and Amenities: Gift shop, Valet service, Barber shop, Beauty shop, Garage and parking, Car hire, Laundry, Complimentary shoeshine, House doctor, Babysitting service on call, Complimentary newspaper, Cable TV, Radio, Telephone, Robes, Whirlpool, Custom-milled soaps and personal care products
Restrictions: No pets; no handicapped access
Concierge: 7:00 a.m.-6:00 p.m.
Room Service: 24 hours
Restaurant: Cafe Mondrian, 7:00 a.m.-10:30 p.m.
Bar: Le Bar, 11:00 a.m.-2:00 a.m.
Business Facilities: Message center, Secretarial service on call, Copiers, Audio-visual, Telex
Conference Rooms: Grand Salon, capacity 100; 3 Boardrooms, capacity 30
Sports Facilities: Heated swimming pool, whirlpool, sauna, aerobics and weight training
Location: West Hollywood

The largest work of art in California, according to the *Los Angeles Herald*, is the facade of The Mondrian Hotel. Painted in 1984 by Israeli artist Yaacov Agam, the work—entitled *Homage a Mondrian*—is 145 feet tall and required 490 gallons of paint in 54 colors. Inside, it's an award winning all-suite luxury hotel.

Each suite consists of living room, kitchenette, wet bar, spacious dressing area and one or two bedrooms. Three telephones in each suite offer teleconference capability. The rooms are done in neutral tones with bright splashes of primary colors after the style of the hotel's namesake, Dutch painter Piet Mondrian. Bathroom amenities include robes, slippers, telephones and a full array of beauty and grooming products. Guests are welcomed to their suites with a basket of fresh fruit. Maid service is twice daily and includes evening turndown.

Sports facilities at The Mondrian include a heated swimming pool, whirlpool spas, complete health club, massage rooms and aerobics classes. There is also a hair styling and skin care salon. The Cafe Mondrian features French California cuisine, along with an impressive view of Los Angeles. The adjoining bar features elegant musical accompaniment nightly.

With its multilingual staff and its pervasive mood of stylish sophistication, Le Mondrian provides full-service hotel facilities centrally located in Los Angeles' entertainment and design community.

THE AHWAHNEE

The Director of the U.S. National Park Service was chagrined when, in 1925, a certain titled English lady declared Yosemite's old Sentinel Hotel "primitive" and refused to stay there. In response, he ordered park concessionaires to construct a modern luxury hotel. Designed by Gilbert Stanley Underwood using massive slabs of native granite stained to the color of redwood, the Ahwahnee Hotel has delighted visitors ever since its opening in July 1927.

The great lounge echos natural magnificence in the giant beams, walk-in fireplaces and floor-to-ceiling windows, with an American Indian decorative motif. After a day exploring the vast grandeur of Yosemite National Park, guests congregate here for afternoon tea and conversation.

Indian designs adorn the door headers, wall trim and hand-blocked bedspreads in the lovely earth-toned guest rooms, and each room contains a serigraph of one of the hotel's Native American baskets or a hand-woven Indian rug.

The main dining room and its adjoining terrace command stupendous views. Thirty-four-foot ceilings complement the granite pillars to create a unique dining atmosphere. The cuisine is All-American with delightful continental and nouveau California influences. A recent autumn dinner opened with Belgian endive salad, then veal medallion with artichoke hearts and lemon sauce, and finally a coup Ahwahnee—meringue filled with Grand Marnier ice cream, raspberries and caramel sauce.

The swimming pool and surrounding grounds provide a most civilized place to bask in Yosemite's wild splendor. Half Dome, Glacier Point, Royal Arches and Yosemite Falls can be viewed from the hotel.

Address: Yosemite National Park 95389
Phone No.: 209-372-1000
Telex: 386211
Reservation Services: Yosemite Park & Curry Co., 209-252-4848
Rates: $$*
Credit Cards: Visa, MC, AmEx, DC
No. of Rooms: 121
Services and Amenities: Gift shop, Valet service, Parking, Baby-sitting service, Laundry, Game area
Restrictions: No pets
Concierge: 9:00 a.m.-5:00 p.m.
Room Service: 7:00 a.m.-10:00 p.m.
Restaurant: Dining Room, 7:00-10:30 a.m., Noon-2:30 p.m., 6:00-8:30 p.m., Dress Code
Bar: Indian Room, Dining Room, Noon-Midnight
Business Facilities: Copiers, Audio-visual
Conference Rooms: 5, capacity 40-100
Sports Facilities: Tennis court, riding, hiking, swimming pool
Location: Yosemite National Park
Attractions: World-famous scenery surrounding hotel

HOTEL JEROME

Address: 330 East Main St., Aspen 81611
Phone No.: 303-920-1000
Toll-free Cable: 800-423-0037 CO, 800-331-7216 US
Rates: $* (Sum.), $$$* (Win.)
Credit Cards: AmEx, Visa, MC
No. of Rooms: 21 **Suites:** 6
Services and Amenities: Valet service, Laundry, Garage and parking, Car hire, Currency exchange, Complimentary shoeshine, House doctor, Baby-sitting service, Complimentary newspaper, TV, Radio, Robe, Whirlpool, Shampoo, Conditioners, Shower cap, Suntan lotion, Facial soap, Toothbrush 7 toothpaste, Razor, Shaving cream, Makeup mirror
Restrictions: Small pets accepted; handicapped access to 2 rooms
Concierge: 8:00-11:00 a.m., 3:00-7:00 p.m.
Room Service: 7:00 a.m.-11:00 p.m.
Restaurant: Silver Queen, 6:00-10:45 p.m.; Jacob's, 7:00 a.m.-3:00 p.m.; Tea Room, 8:00 a.m.-10:00 p.m.; MTV Room, 4:00 p.m.-1:00 a.m.
Bar: Jacob's Bar, 7:00 a.m.-11:00 p.m.; Jerome Bar, 11:00 a.m.-2:00 a.m.
Business Facilities: Message center, Secretarial service, Translators, Copiers, Audio-visual, Teleconferencing, Telex
Conference Rooms: 2, capacity 100
Sports Facilities: 7 outdoor & 3 indoor tennis courts, 3 squash courts, 7 racquetball courts, riding, polo, golf, sailing, skiing
Attractions: Boutique shopping, Aspen Music Festival, art galleries, Aspen Institute, Maroon Lake

The Jerome was originally built in 1899 as the centerpiece of Aspen, the "Silver Queen of the Rockies." The hotel has recently been expanded and renovated to surpass even its original grandeur. The interior has been restored in East Lake gothic, a style at once lively, colorful, and delicate, with florals, tendrils and oriental flourishes. Designers Charles T. Mayhew of Raleigh Interior Design and Zoe Murphy of Aspen Furniture Design have accomplished the extraordinary in integrating many of the original decorative elements. Each spacious, comfortable guest room is a masterpiece, and no two are alike. Features include original antiques, brass beds, fine fabrics and exquisite wall coverings. The baths have black-and-white tile floors, Jacuzzi bathtubs with separate showers, double sinks with period fixtures and Italian marble vanities. The 500-square-foot grand parlor suite, with its lavish turn-of-the-century decor, features a large fireplace, wet bar, guest bath, walk-in closet and armoires concealing TVs in both the parlor and the bathroom.

The Silver Queen restaurant, in burgundy velvet with Italian tapestries, provides a plush formal Victorian setting. The cuisine is marvelous. Be sure to try the Avocado Jerome and, as an entree, the swordfish with orange and ginger sauce. The dessert souffles are a house specialty. Afternoon tea, pastries and cocktails are served in the three-story atrium lobby.

The lively Jerome bar has a rustic decor featuring the original bar, lamps and 1890s furnishings. While enjoying the convivial atmosphere, why not sample the house specialty, Coffee Jerome?

Bravo to Dick Butera for his foresight and tenacity in rescuing this once-grand lady from decrepitude to its present world-class beauty and elegance.

OXFORD HOTEL

Downtown Denver's oldest grand hotel, the Oxford opened in 1891 at the peak of Colorado's silver bonanza. The elegant Victorian brick structure, now listed on the National Register of Historic Places, reopened in 1983 after remarkably authentic restoration from the original blueprints.

The 82 rooms and suites are individually appointed with lovely English and French antiques. In the baths, 19th-Century tiles and clawfoot tubs mix well with such modern amenities as telephones, robes and luxury toiletries. Evening turndown service is sweetened with a Godiva chocolate on the pillow, and complimentary breakfast is brought to your room along with the morning newspaper.

The prestigious Oxford Club restaurant is open only to hotel guests and club members. Dishes such as roast rack of Colorado lamb with honey glaze and fresh rosemary, and sauteed Colorado trout with macadamia nuts, make up the bill of fare. The wine list is outstanding. On a more casual note, the hotel's other fine restaurant, The Sage, has the ambience of a European cafe. The Cruise Room bar, itself on the National Register, is an authentic art deco gem with rose neon lights, velvet covered booths and marble floors. Who can resist?

In keeping with the hotel's Victorian charm is the custom of serving complimentary sherry and biscuits on each floor from 5:00 to 7:00 p.m.

Guests wishing to "work out" are extended privileges to the International Athletic Club. Within walking distance are historic Larimer Square, the Center for the Performing Arts and Denver's financial district.

Address: 1600 Seventeenth St., Denver 80202
Phone No.: 303-627-5400
Toll-free Cable: 800-228-5838
Telex: 910-931-0413
Reservation Services: 800-223-0888
Rates: $$*
Credit Cards: AmEx, Choice, Visa, MC, DC
No. of Rooms: 81 **Suites:** 10
Services and Amenities: Valet service, Barber shop, Beauty shop, Garage and parking, Complimentary shoeshine, House doctor, Baby-sitting service, Complimentary vintage limousine service, Complimentary newspaper, TV, Radio, Telephones, Robes, Complimentary toiletries
Restrictions: No pets; no handicapped access
Concierge: 8:00 a.m.-5:00 p.m.
Room Service: 24 hours
Restaurant: The Oxford Club & The Sage, 6:30 a.m.-10:30 p.m., Dress Code
Bar: The Cruise Room, 11:00 a.m.-2:00 a.m.
Business Facilities: Complete business service center
Conference Rooms: 8, capacity 150
Sports Facilities: Aerobics and weight training, access to International Athletic Club
Location: Downtown near theatres
Attractions: Symphony and theatres

GOVERNORS COURT HOTEL

Address: 1776 Grant St., Denver 80203
Phone No.: 303-861-2000
Toll-free Cable: 800-525-2888 outside Colorado
Reservation Services: Registry/HMC 214-248-4300
Rates: $$*
Credit Cards: AmEx, Visa, MC, DC
No. of Rooms: 193 **Suites:** 44
Services and Amenities: Gift shop, Laundry, Valet service, Garage and parking free to hotel guests, Car hire, Baby-sitting service, TV, Radio, Shampoo, Lotion, Shoeshine hand glove, Specialized Soap
Restrictions: No Pets; handicapped access to 10 rooms
Concierge: 7:00 a.m.-10:00 p.m.
Room Service: 6:30 a.m.-10:30 p.m.
Restaurant: Governor's Table, 6:30 a.m.-10:30 p.m.
Bar: Club at the Court, 11:00 a.m.-1:00 a.m.
Business Facilities: Message center, Secretarial service, Copiers
Conference Rooms: 6, capacity 250
Sports Facilities: Swimming pool
Location: Downtown
Attractions: Sixteenth Street Shopping Mall, Denver and Western Art Museums, State Capitol

This modern high-rise of maroon-colored brick is located in downtown Denver's capital district, within easy walking distance of the Museum of Art. Fine wood furnishings and a tasteful earth-tone color scheme contribute to the civilized and fashionable atmosphere.

The spacious rooms, in hues of navy blue, forest green or muted rust, feature brass and mahogany furniture. Bathrooms, too, are oversized and most have telephones. A favorite suite, the Symphony, has an elegant separate living area with an 1817 piano, a glass-topped mahogany table with eight chairs, chandeliers, a wet bar and one-and-a-half baths. The green marble master bathroom has a giant black bathtub and sitting area. The bedroom has an enormous step-up bed, as well as a game table with two leather chairs for that impromptu bout of backgammon.

The Governors Court caters particularly to traveling executives. In addition to conference facilities, enticements include complimentary limousine service to downtown-area destinations, a concierge on duty from 7 a.m. to 10 p.m., and the pleasant custom of afternoon cocktails and complimentary hors d'oeuvres after the day's work.

The rooftop pool affords views of downtown and the mountains. Next door is a health club spa, to which guests are extended privileges, with racquet ball, bicycle room and aerobics.

The Governors Table restaurant offers fine continental cuisine in a traditional setting. On a recent evening, a delicious dinner included cold antipasto salad, French onion soup, sorbet, pepperloin St. Louis, dalphine potatoes and, for dessert, a poached pear with Grand Marnier custard. The Club at the Court features an elegant long bar, ceiling fans and a slate floor.

The management and staff here work hard to provide a warm, friendly atmosphere to make their guests feel at home away from home.

THE LODGE AT VAIL

Vail, best known as a winter sports paradise with America's most extensive ski slopes, has fine summer sports possibilities as well: tennis, horseback riding, golf, whitewater rafting and more. The Lodge at Vail offers complete recreation and dining facilities, including a heated pool, Jacuzzis and three restaurants. The Alpine atmosphere prevails throughout the resort.

The rooms and suites are individually decorated with lovely mahogany wood panelling, floral bedspreads and draperies, and carpeting in signature grey, pink and cream. The baths have marble counters, telephones, hair dryers and, as an unusual touch, heated towel racks.

Room service is available 24 hours a day. The international staff's meticulous attention to even the smallest details ensures each guest a pleasurable stay.

Walking into the Wildflower Inn, the primary dining room, is like entering a spring garden in full bloom. The tables are set with Villeroy and Boch china, Reed & Barton silver, Zwissel crystal, and Laura Ashley table linens. A typical dinner might consist of roast oysters served warm with mignett arugula, with Puilly Fume wine; fresh field salad with roast garlic dressing; veal osso bucco; Acacia Pinot Noir wine; and for dessert, Tiramisu.

The rustic bar, Mickey's, offers a toasty fire, live music, the warming house drink Coffee Amadeus—and the best of Vail's world-famous apres-ski social scene.

Address: 174 East Gore Creek Drive, Vail 81657
Phone No.: 303-476-5011
Telex: 45-0375
Reservation Service: HRI, 800-223-6800
Rates: $$$*
Credit Cards: All major credit cards
No. of Rooms: 222 **Suites:** 88
Services and Amenities: Gift shop, Laundry, Valet service, Garage and parking, Car hire, International currency exchange, Complimentary shoeshine, House doctor on call, Baby-sitting service, Marble counters, Full-view mirrors, Telephones, Hair dryers, Heated towel racks, Full line of amenities packaged for the Lodge
Restrictions: No pets; no handicapped access
Concierge: All day
Room Service: 24 hours
Restaurant: Wildflower Inn, Tue.-Sun.; Cafe Arlberg, 7:30 a.m.-11:00 p.m.
Bar: Mickey's, 4:00 p.m.-2:00 a.m.
Business Facilities: Message center, Secretarial service on request, Translators, Copiers, Audio-visual, Teleconferencing, Telex
Conference Rooms: 5
Sports Facilities: 6 asphalt tennis courts, 2 golf courses, skiing, riding, sailing, river rafting, ice skating, fishing, swimming pool
Location: Vail Village
Attractions: American Ski Classic, 1989 World Ski Championships, balloon races, Coors Classic bike race, Jerry Ford Invitational Kiva Tennis Classic

VAIL ATHLETIC CLUB

Vail Athletic Club & Hotel
Address: 352 E. Meadow Drive, Vail 81657
Phone No.: 303-476-0700
Toll-free Cable: 800-VACH-SKI
Telex: 317720
Reservation Services: Vail Resort Assoc., 303-476-1000
Rates: $ (Sum.), $$* (Win.)
Credit Cards: MC, Visa, AmEx
No. of Rooms: 40 **Suites:** 7
Services and Amenities: Laundry, Valet service, Barber shop, Beauty shop, Car hire, Baby-sitting service, Complimentary newspaper, Cable TV, Radio, Telephone, Robes, Soap, Shampoo, Creme rinse, Shower cap, Sun protector, ChapStick, Shoeshine cloth
Restrictions: No pets, handicapped access to 40 rooms
Room Service: 6:30 a.m.-10:00 p.m. (winter)
Restaurant: Maison Creole, 7:00 a.m.-10:00 p.m. (winter)
Bar: Mardi Gras Lounge, 4:00 p.m.-10.30 p.m.
Business Facilities: Message center, Secretarial service, Copiers, Audio-visual, Teleconferencing, Telex
Conference Rooms: 3, capacity 15-20-50
Sports Facilities: Swimming pool, handball, squash, croquet, rafting, fishing, cycling, hiking, skiing 2 blocks, full health spa
Location: Downtown
Attractions: Unique shops, sports, jazz festivals, historic tours

As its name implies, the sporting life is the Vail Athletic Club & Hotel's *raison d'etre.* All ski lifts and gondolas are close by, and the hotel has its own outstanding Human Performance Center with professional staff including two doctors, a nurse and a nutritionist. The guest rooms are luxuriously appointed in hues of mauve, peach and seafoam green. Each room has a humidifier and terry cloth robes. Most have splendid Rocky Mountain views.

Upon arrival, each guest is greeted with a box of Godiva chocolates. You can work them off later in the spa.

The Maison Creole, a New Orleans type restaurant, has taken Vail by storm. Dinner may begin with an hors d'oeuvre of barbecued shrimp in the shell, followed by blackened redfish (grilled filet of redfish seasoned piquant and served with burned lemon butter). The house drink, Cappucino d'Amour, is best enjoyed by the sunken fireplace in the Mardi Gras Lounge.

The staff is ready to assist you in arranging your Rocky Mountain experience, be it wintertime skiing, snowmobiling and sleigh rides, or summertime rafting, fishing and hiking in the Gore Wilderness.

INN AT MILL RIVER

Connecticut's newest and most intimate luxury hotel overlooks a tranquil river, yet is just minutes by hotel limousine from major corporate centers and less than one hour from New York City. Theatres and excellent shopping are within walking distance.
With only 92 rooms and suites, the Inn at Mill River combines the ambience and hospitality of a private manor with the sophistication and service of a metropolitan hotel. The spacious, casual guest rooms are furnished in Old English, Louis XV and contemporary styles. Superb original artwork and antiques endow each room with individual character. The rooms have fine linens, down pillows and comforters, and delightful baths fitted out with terry robes, plush towels and French toiletries. Internationally renowned designer James Northcutt's hand is evident throughout the Inn. The Swan Court restaurant offers formal dining with table settings of hand-blown crystal and Wedgewood china. The classic French cuisine features such specialties as quail pate, Dover sole en croute, and chocolate terrine.
In the Library, guests congregate to enjoy afternoon tea, after-dinner port and cordials. The delightful ambience of the Cygnet bar is enhanced by raw silk couches, deep pillows and harp music. Guests enjoy privileges to the Landmark Health Club, a full service spa.
For executive guests, the Inn's private salons provide a richly appointed, professional working environment. The Boardroom features an elegant eighteen-seat inlaid mahogany conference table and a private courtyard.

Address: 26 Mill River Street, Stamford 06902
Phone No.: 203-325-1900
Toll-free Cable: 800-325-0345 US
Reservation Services: Preferred Hotels
Rates: $$*
Credit Cards: AmEx, Visa, MC
No. of Rooms: 94 **Suites:** 14
Services and Amenities: Laundry, Valet service, Library, Garage and parking, Car hire, Complimentary shoeshine, House doctor, Baby-sitting service, Complimentary newspaper, Cable TV, Radio, Telephone, Robes, Skin moisturizer, Shampoo, Shower cap, Shoehorn and cloth, Emeryboard
Restrictions: No pets; handicapped access to 4 rooms
Concierge: 7:00 a.m.-11:00 p.m.
Room Service: 7:00 a.m.-11:00 p.m.
Restaurant: The Swan Court, Noon-10:00 p.m.; Promenade, 7:00 a.m.-10:00 a.m.; Dress Code
Bar: Cygnet, Noon-1:00 a.m.
Business Facilities: Message center, Secretarial service, Audio-visual, Copiers
Conference Rooms: 2, capacity 10-75
Sports Facilities: Automatic membership in Landmark Health Club, full health spa, whirlpool, sauna, massage, aerobics, weight training
Location: Downtown theatre district
Attractions: Landmark Square and Stamford Town Center, 5 min. to Palace and Hartman theatres, Stamford Center for the Performing Arts

HOTEL DU PONT

Address: 11th & Market St., Wilmington 19899
Phone No.: 302-594-3100
Telex: 905015 du Pont Hotel
Reservation Services: Preferred Hotels, 800-323-7500
Rates: $$*
Credit Cards: Visa, MC, AmEx, DC, CB
No. of Rooms: 266 **Suites:** 5
Services and Amenities: Laundry, Valet service, Barber shop, Beauty shop, Garage and parking, Car hire, International currency exchange, House doctor, Baby-sitting service, Complimentary newspaper with room service, Telephone, TV, Customized guest amenities
Restrictions: No pets; handicapped access to 2 rooms
Concierge: 9:00 a.m.-6:00 p.m.
Room Service: 7:00 a.m.-11:00 p.m.
Restaurant: Green Room or Brandywine Room, Dress Code
Bar: Lobby Lounge, 11:00 a.m.-1:00 p.m.
Business Facilities: Message center, Secretarial service, Copiers, Audio-visual, Telex
Conference Rooms: 5, capacity 8-80
Sports Facilities: Tennis can be arranged
Location: Center city
Attractions: Winterthur Museum and Gardens, Longwood Gardens, Brandywine River Museum, Hagley Museum

Hotel du Pont has been under the continuous ownership of E. I. du Pont de Nemours Company since it opened its doors in 1913. This *ne plus ultra* corporate showpiece has hosted several kings, many ambassadors and thousands of other famous personages from around the world.

In the Brandywine Valley, midway between New York and Washington DC, the Hotel du Pont is only 25 miles from the Philadelphia International Airport. 24-hour airport shuttle service is provided. The lobby's unique high-relief ceiling, tall arched windows and original art work are typical of the superb craftsmanship evidenced throughout the hotel. The guest rooms, elegantly appointed with Queen Anne furnishings, have a residential feel. The large suites are decorated in a palette of soft pastel colors and accented with crystal lamps, chandeliers and period antiques.

The cuisine in both the Green Room and the Brandywine Restaurant is classically prepared and served with flair. Specialties include a mushroom and crabmeat imperial hors d'oeuvre, seafood Christina prepared at your table, and various hot dessert souffles. Private dining rooms, with gold place settings, Waterford crystal and lace table cloths, are also available.

Guests are extended privileges at the du Pont Country Club. The Winterthur Museum and Gardens, home of the world's most comprehensive collection of early American decorative art and antiques, is a short drive from the hotel, as are the Brandywine River Museum, the Hagley Museum, and the magnificent 350-acre Longwood Gardens.

THE REACH

At once gently Victorian and boldly sensual, this tropical retreat creates its own unique sense of time and place. The new pink and white complex, lush with palms and flowers, commands Key West's only private natural beach.

Guest rooms are done in island-inspired pine with cane furnishings, marble-topped nightstands and ceiling fans. Special features include Indian dhurrie rugs, Mexican floor tiles, Japanese kimonos and an ingenious coffee mill-brewer with a timer that will awaken you each morning to its tantalizing aroma.

The Celebration restaurant serves "New American" cuisine in gazebos on a terrace suspended above the ocean. Emma's bistro offers exotic fare from Thailand, Singapore, the Mississippi Delta and the Caribbean, and features live island jazz until 2 a.m. Tea, sherry and port are served in the library—by the librarian.

The range of sporting facilities and activities includes a huge swimming pool, health club, sailboats, catamarans, paddleboats, windsurfing, snorkeling or simply basking in the sunshine on one of Florida's finest beaches.

Address: 1435 Simonton at the Ocean, Key West 33040
Phone No.: 305-296-5000
Reservation Service: 800-874-4118
Rates: $$*
Credit Cards: Visa, MC, DC, AmEx
No. of Rooms: 150 **Suites:** 80
Services and Amenities: Gift shop, Laundry, Valet service, Library, Garage and parking, Car hire, Baby-sitting service, Game area, Cable TV, Telephone, Robes, Stocked mini-bars, Key West suntan gel, Shampoo, Face cream, Bath gel
Restrictions: No pets; handicapped access to 8 rooms
Concierge: 8:00 a.m.-8:00 p.m.
Room Service: 24 hours
Restaurant: Celebration, 5:30-11:00 p.m.; Emma's, 7:00 a.m.-2:00 a.m.
Bar: Emma's, Celebration, Nightfall, Sandbar, Lobby, 10:00 a.m.-2:00 a.m.
Business Facilities: Secretarial service, Copiers, Audio-visual, Telex, Message center
Conference Rooms: 5, capacity 280
Sports Facilities: Swimming pool, tennis courts available 3 min., golf available 5 min., sailing
Location: Edge of old town on the beach
Attractions: Hemingway house, Mel Fisher's $400 million treasure trove, deep-sea fishing, Tennessee Williams Festival

HAWK'S CAY

Address: Mile Marker 61, Marathon 33050
Phone No.: 305-743-7000
Toll-free Cable: 800-327-7775
Rates: $$*
Credit Cards: Visa, MC, AmEx
No. of Rooms: 178 **Suites:** 16
Services and Amenities: Library, Baby-sitting service, Game area, Parking, Laundry, Complimentary newspaper, Cable TV, Telephone, Shampoo, Lotions
Restrictions: No pets; handicapped access to 1 room and public areas
Concierge: 8:30 a.m.-7:30 p.m. daily
Room Service: Yes
Restaurant: The Caribbean Room, 6:00-11:00 p.m.; Ship's Galley, dockside
Bar: Cantina Lounge and Ship's Pub, 11:00 a.m.-2:00 a.m.
Business Facilities: Message center, Secretarial service, Spanish translators, Copiers, Audio-visual
Conference Rooms: 8
Sports Facilities: 2 lighted clay tennis courts, 6 hard-surface tennis courts, croquet, sailing, golf nearby, swimming pool
Location: Resort area
Attractions: Fishing and diving capital, boutiques, Key West 1 hour away

Dolphins cavort in their own private lagoon at Hawk's Cay Resort. No, we're not referring to Miami's football superstars. Hawk's Cay hosts the training/feeding facility where both dolphins and sea lions rehearse their roles for water shows throughout America, to the delight of the resort's human guests.

Built in the late 1950's and completely renovated in 1983, the rambling 178-room West Indies style hotel sits in the middle of its own private island. Guests here have included three presidents as well as many Hollywood notables.

Charter fishing excursions from the hotel's marina offer some of the world's best big-game fishing. Marlin, wahoo and tuna are plentiful, and the resort record sailfish catch weighed in at 83 pounds. Other activities include skin diving, snorkeling, sailing and bicycling. The tennis courts are surrounded by tropical gardens, and the nearby 18-hole Sombrero Golf Course extends membership privileges to guests.

The four restaurants at Hawk's Cay serve superb fresh-from-the-sea fish dinners. In the Caribbean Room, a delectable specialty is tournedos smothered with crab meat and covered with choron And for dessert—key lime pie, of course.

With four large meeting rooms, Hawk's Cay is ideally equipped for conferences.

TURNBERRY ISLE

A total resort environment secluded on a 300-acre island just off North Miami Beach, Turnberry's own little world combines privacy, fabulous recreational facilities, gourmet dining and glamorous night life.

The resort includes three separate hotels. The Marina Hotel at the yacht harbor entrance is styled after the most intimate, ultra-elite Mediterranean hideaways. The Country Club Hotel fronts the subtropical gardens, manicured lawns and winding waterways of Turnberry Fairways. The Yacht Club Hotel lies at the entrance to one of America's premier yachting facilities.

The spacious rooms in each hotel are exquisitely decorated in the peach-and-blue Turnberry color scheme. Wide terraces provide panoramic views of the marina and grounds. The deluxe 1600-square-foot suites feature hand-tiled bars, solariums with redwood hot tubs, and baths with oversized Jacuzzis, plentiful beauty and grooming products and Evian water.

Sports facilities abound: twenty-four lighted tennis courts with a professional teaching staff headed by Fred Stolle (coach to Jimmy Connors and Vitas Gerulitis); two Robert Trent Jones 18-hole golf courses; and the fully protected 125-slip marina. The Ocean Park Club has Camelot-like tented cabanas, pool, beach front bar, seaside cafe and lounges. Wind surfing, Hobicat and diving gear rentals are available on site. The Turnberry Spa, among the world's most lavish dens of self-indulgence, offers racquetball courts, sauna and steam baths, beauty salon, Swiss jet showers and much more. After dark the Turnberry Disco pulses to irresistible rhythms.

In the formal Monaco Dining Room, a recent dinner featured juicy beefsteak tomatoes with fresh mozzarella and sweet onions, baked sea bass with grilled fennel, and a hot Grand Marnier souffle.

Extensive meeting facilities are geared to the needs of an international clientele.

Turnberry is graced with many spectacular works of art. Be sure to see Giacometti's *La Grand Femme*, one of our very favorites.

Turnberry Isle Yacht & Country Club
Address: 19735 Turnberry Way, Miami 33180
Phone No.: 305-932-6200
Toll-free Cable: 800-327-7028
Rates: $
Credit Cards: AmEx, CB, DC, MC, Visa
No. of Rooms: 111 **Suites:** 23
Services and Amenities: Valet service, Barber shop, Beauty shop, Laundry, Garage and parking, Car hire, Complimentary shoeshine, House doctor, Baby-sitting service, Gift shop, Safe, Jacuzzi, Bidet, Complimentary newspaper, Cable TV, Robes, VCR, Audio cassette player, Radio, Complimentary toiletries
Restrictions: No pets
Concierge: 24 hours
Room Service: 24 hours
Restaurant: Monaco Dining Room, Country Club Dining Room, 8:00 a.m.-Midnight, Dress Code
Bar: Celebrity Lounge/Monaco Lounge, 11:00 a.m.-2:00 a.m.
Business Facilities: Business services available on request. Message center, Secretarial service, Translators, Copiers, Audio-visual, Teleconferencing, Telex
Conference Rooms: 6, 13,000 square feet
Sports Facilities: 24 tennis courts, racquetball, golf courses (36 holes), sailing, health spa, fishing, whirlpool, sauna, massage, aerobics, weight training
Attractions: Racetracks, jai alai, shopping, Villa Viscaya, Coconut Grove

GRAND BAY HOTEL

Address: 2669 S. Bayshore Dr., Coconut Grove 33133
Phone No.: 305-858-9600
Telex: 441370 GBHUI
Reservation Services: 800-221-2340
Rates: $$$*
Credit Cards: All major credit cards
No. of Rooms: 122 **Suites:** 59
Services and Amenities: Valet service, Barber shop, Beauty shop, Laundry, Garage and parking, Car hire, Currency exchange, Complimentary shoeshine, House doctor, Baby-sitting service, Gift shop, Complimentary newspaper, Cable TV, Radio, Robes, Complimentary toiletries
Restrictions: No pets; no handicapped access
Concierge: 24 hours
Restaurant: Grand Cafe, 7:00 a.m.-3:00 p.m., 6:30-11:00 p.m., Dress Code; Regine's (private club for members and hotel guests only), 8:00 p.m.-Midnight, Dress Code
Bar: CIGA Lounge
Business Facilities: Many business services available on request
Conference Rooms: 7, capacity 20-400
Sports Facilities: Health club with sauna, massage, weight training, on Marina with access to water sports
Location: Coconut Grove, 15 min. from airport, airport transportation on request
Attractions: Shopping, Vizcaya, Key Biscayne, Downtown Miami, Seaquarium, Planet Ocean, Mayfair shops

If the ultimate in style and a "jet set" social scene appeal to you, you will love the Grand Bay. The first American hotel to be developed by the Italian firm CIGA, the Grand Bay Hotel is Miami *par excellence.*

Interior designer Diane Sepler, working with the Nichols Partnership architects, has created a modern classic extravaganza. From the distinctive pyramidal architecture to the rooftop nightclub, Regine's, with its international superstar clientele, this is a hotel to write home about.

You may be welcomed with a bottle of French champagne, or with cut flowers and a personal note from the manager. Guest rooms, with views of Biscayne Bay and the Coconut Grove Marina, are decorated in soft peach tones with a country French theme. Each room has a fully-stocked wet bar. Baths are supplied with an alluring array of toiletries.

The Grand Cafe is light, airy and sophisticated. Such delights as she-crab soup, black linguini with calamari, and chocolate truffle terrine keep guests coming back for more. Round-the-clock room service makes the entire Grand Cafe menu available at your whim.

The nightlife at Regine's is the liveliest in Coconut Grove, and perhaps in the entire Miami area. The style and energy are extraordinary, and the decor reminds one of a mirrored raspberry velvet jewel box.

A chauffeured limousine awaits to take you downtown for business appointments or shopping.

SEA GODDESS CRUISES

No survey of the United States' most elegant accommodations would be complete without mentioning the ultimate in floating pleasure palaces—the Miami-based Sea Goddess Cruises. Sea Goddesses I and II roam the world, their agendas varying by season to include the Caribbean, the Mediterranean, Egypt and Israel, and South American ports of call; wherever they may be bound, the two Sea Goddess ships offer an unrivaled ambience of opulence afloat.

All guest quarters are surprisingly spacious suites, lavishly decorated with emphasis on fine fabrics and natural textures. Each suite has a wet bar, radio and television with VCR, and there is a large library of videotapes aboard. All staterooms have full baths complete with robes, luxury toiletries and sunlamps.

The dining salon, its tables laid in classic French crystal and silver, delights the eye. Dinner is sumptuous, stylish and relaxed—no hurried regimentation here, and if you wish you may choose your own table. The imaginative cuisine blends French Nouvelle with new American. Cocktails, liqueurs and most wines are complimentary. Breakfast and lunch are served *al fresco* in the delightful outdoor cafe. Full room service is available 24 hours a day.

A regal yachting experience in every subtlest detail, the Sea Goddess lifestyle defies comparison with any other adventure on earth.

Address: 5850 Blue Lagoon Drive, Miami 33126
Phone No.: 305-266-8705
Toll-free Cable: 800-475-9000, 800-458-9000
Telex: 264502 USM UR
Rates: $$$$*
Credit Cards: MC, Visa, DC for on-board purchases only
Suites: 58
Services and Amenities: Valet service, Library, Laundry, Barber shop, Beauty shop, Car hire, Complimentary shoeshine, House doctor, Game area, Complimentary newspaper, Cable TV, VCR, Radio, Telephone, Robes, Sun lamp, Complimentary toiletries
Restrictions: No pets; no handicapped access; children full-rate
Concierge: 24 hours
Room Service: 24 hours
Restaurant: Dining Salon, Outdoor cafe
Business Facilities: Message center, Copiers, Audio-visual, Teleconferencing, Telex
Sports Facilities: Available in many ports of call: handball/squash, croquet, golf, sailing, windsurfing, water skiing, swimming
Attractions: Cruises-Caribbean, Mediteranean, Egypt and Israel, South America

GOVERNORS INN

Address: 209 South Adams Street, Tallahassee 32301
Phone No.: 904-681-6855
Toll-free Cable: 800-342-7717 (Florida only)
Rates: $
Credit Cards: AmEx, DC, CB, Visa, MC
No. of Rooms: 41 **Suites:** 6
Services and Amenities: Valet service, Library, Garage and parking, Baby-sitting service, Card game area, Continental breakfast & cocktails, Complimentary newspaper of choice, Cable TV, Telephone, Robes, Bath soap, Hand soap, Shampoo, Shower cap
Restrictions: No pets
Room Service: 11:30 a.m.-2:00 p.m., 6:00 p.m.-10:00 p.m.
Restaurant: Golden Pheasant, Mon.-Fri. lunch 11:30 a.m.-2:00 p.m., Dinner 6:00-10:00 p.m., Sat. dinner only; Dress Code
Business Facilities: Message center, Secretarial service, Translators, Copiers
Conference Rooms: 2, capacity 12-75
Location: Adams Street Common
Attractions: Central City, ½ block north of Capitol building

A renovated building in the center of the Adams Street Common, one-half block from the state capitol, the Governors Inn combines original woodwork, exposed beams and brilliant skylights to create a French country environment.

The 41 guest rooms and suites are furnished with antique armoires and English pub tables. Some have French four-poster beds and framed prints depicting Florida's plants, birds and shells. No two rooms are alike. The Spessard Holland suite, for example, has an ample parlor with wet bar, vaulted ceilings, oversized windows and king-sized bed, and overlooks the Common. Other rooms feature loft bedrooms and fireplaces, spiral staircases and clerestory windows. Large bathrooms are equipped with telephones, robes and many personal care amenities.

The elegant Golden Pheasant French restaurant is a Tallahassee favorite. A salmon and powder blue color scheme sets the stage for fine cuisine. Assorted pates and terrines are among the house specialties. Try the roast rack of lamb with honey and mustard sauce, with marjolaine for dessert.

Many guests here are corporate executives visiting the capital on business, and the hotel's professional staff can help arrange for conferences of any size up to 75 people.

THE CLOISTER

Five miles of private beach and 10,000 acres of surrounding forest and marsh make this sunny sub-tropical island playground a paradise for honeymooners, family vacationers and sports enthusiasts. The Spanish-architecture resort complex, built in 1928, offers accommodations in the main hotel, the River House, and an array of guesthouses and beach cottages. Lodging locations and sizes vary considerably, and rates adjust accordingly.

The entire property is a garden a-bloom the year around. Flowers grace the tables and the rooms. The food is superb—from the exquisite club buffet to breakfast served on your own private balcony overlooking the ocean. The Cloister orchestra plays nightly for dancing.

The sporting life reigns supreme. America's finest golf is to be found here, with 54 championship holes designed by Walter Travis on what were once the cotton fields of an antebellum seaside plantation. Guests can also enjoy clubhouse facilities at two excellent country clubs, as well as 18 fast-dry clay tennis courts, two pools at Sea Island Beach Club, three skeet fields and a trap field at the Gun Club, bicycles, fishing, inland cruising boats and ocean sailboats, and horses for ring, trail or beach riding.

There are exceptional conference facilities, and The Cloister sponsors frequent financial management seminars, art shows and many activities especially for children.

Address: Sea Island 31561
Phone No.: 912-638-3611
Toll-free Cable: 800-732-4752
Rates: $$$*
No. of Rooms: 264 **Suites:** 100
Services and Amenities: Gift shop, Laundry, Valet service, Barber shop, Beauty shop, Garage and parking, Car hire, Baby-sitting service, Games area, Cable TV, Telephone
Restrictions: No pets; handicapped access to 6 rooms
Concierge: 7:00 a.m.-9:00 p.m.
Room Service: 7:00 a.m.-9:00 p.m.
Restaurant: The Cloister Dining Rooms
Bar: Several, open all day
Business Facilities: Message center, Secretarial service, Copiers, Audio-visual
Conference Rooms: 12, capacity 350
Sports Facilities: 18 fast dry tennis courts, croquet, 54 holes of golf, riding, sailing, skeet and trap shooting, boating and fishing, bicycling, 2 swimming pools
Location: on 5-mile beach

KAPALUA BAY HOTEL

Kapalua Bay Hotel & Villas
Address: One Bay Drive, Kapalua 96761
Phone Nos.: 800-367-3000, 800-669-5656
Telex: ITT 669-6515$
Rates: $$$*
Credit Cards: AmEx, Visa, MC, CB, DC
No. of Rooms: 194 **Suites:** 3
Services and Amenities: Valet service, Barber shop, Beauty shop, Garage and parking, Car hire, Laundry, Currency exchange, Baby-sitting service, Cable TV, Shampoo, Conditioners, Robes
Restrictions: No pets; handicapped access to 2 rooms
Concierge: 8:00 a.m.-6:00 p.m.
Room Service: 6:45 a.m.-10:00 p.m.
Restaurant: The Plantation Veranda, 6:30-10:00 p.m.; The Bay Club; The Garden-Dress Code
Bar: The Bay Lounge, 4:30-8:30 p.m.
Business Facilities: Message center, Secretarial service, Audio-visual, Copiers, Teleconferencing, Telex
Conference Rooms: 2, capacity 15; 1, capacity 100
Sports Facilities: 10 Plexi-pave tennis courts, 36 holes golf, sailing, aerobics
Location: 7 mi. from Lahaina, 40 mi. from Kahului Airport, Maui

On the northwest tip of Maui, above white sand beaches sheltered by lava peninsulas, with the neighboring islands of Lanai and Molokai visible across the brilliant blue waters of the bay, nestles a 750-acre tropical paradise certain to delight even the most demanding international traveler.

Kapalua Bay Hotel and Villas is a full service resort with three secluded beaches, 36 holes of golf designed by Arnold Palmer, and a tennis garden with ten plexi-pave courts arranged in separate pairs to eliminate distractions. Beside the hotel is a gallery of 22 unique international boutiques and shops.

The spacious guest rooms are done in relaxing pastels, with natural wood accents throughout. Each air-conditioned room has a private sitting area and lanai. The baths have "his-and-her" amenities and oversized dressing areas.

The Plantation Veranda, one of several fine dining options, is elegantly decorated with Pegge Hopper murals on the walls. Ceiling fans do a slow dance overhead. Special touches like complimentary royale kir and an orchid spray for every lady complement the lovely environment. A harpist plays nightly. Your divine dinner might begin with pates or melon in strawberry liqueur, followed by a Plantation salad. Seafood may be poached with saffron and tomatoes or sauteed with lobster and Beurre Blanc. From the Kiawe charcoal grill come noisettes of spring lamb in tomato coulis and chanterelles. A fresh tropical fruit sorbet ends the meal on a note of perfection.

Other dining choices include the pool terrace and the Bar with its sporty atmosphere. The wine list here is a connoisseur's dream. The Bay Lounge offers tea service from 3:00 to 5:00 and hors d'oeuvres thereafter. The lounge is ideal for sunset views, best appreciated with the aid of the house specialty drink, the Kapalua Butterfly.

Internationally renowned since it opened in 1978, the Kapalua Bay hotel is the centerpiece of an award winning community and a remarkable hotel experience not to be missed.

After all, where else can you watch whales cavorting from your terrace?

HANA MAUI

The lovely Hotel Hana Maui is in the exclusive, secluded Hana area of the island of Maui. Eighty-two bungalow style accommodations are scattered throughout 23 acres of landscaped gardens within a 4,500-acre working ranch.

James Northcutt Associates, interior designers, have created a striking decor in white with natural wood beams and Bermuda shutters. Plantation ceiling fans whir overhead, aided by air conditioning if you desire. Orchids and other tropical plants bloom indoors as well as out. The luxurious baths have sunken tubs, and outside each bath is an enclosed private garden.

The sporting life is in full swing at the Hana Maui. Facilities include a large heated swimming pool, tennis courts, croquet lawn and well-equipped riding stable. Scuba diving and a full range of water sports are available at the beach.

The Hotel Hana Maui is justly renowned. The atmosphere is casual. Be sure to try the filet of mahi mahi steamed in lime with fresh fennel and citrus butter, and the macadamia nut pie.

Paniolo Bar is a favorite meeting spot for low-key casual "elegant ranch atmosphere" and great drinks such as the Hana Ho and Mai Tai.

The Hana area is rich in Hawaiian lore and replete with things to do and see. View the botanical gardens, enjoy the hiking trails in 120 acre Waianapanapa State Park and the Seven Pools at Ohe'o, and don't miss the world's largest stone *heiau*, an ancient place of worship. To stay at the Hana Maui is to experience "where old Hawaii lives."

Address: Post Office 8 (I), Hana, Maui 96713

Phone No.: 808-248-8211
Telex: HANAHO

Reservation Service: John A. Tetley Co., CA 800-252-0211, US 800-421-0000

Rates: $$$$*

Credit Cards: Visa, MC, AmEx

Services and Amenities: Valet service, Library, Beauty shop, Car hire, International currency exchange, Complimentary shoeshine, Laundry, House doctor upon request, Baby-sitting service, Game area, Bath telephone, Robes, Shell soap, Shower caps

Restrictions: No pets

Concierge: Activities desk, 7:00 a.m.-6:00 p.m.

Restaurant: Hotel Hana-Maui Restaurant, 6:30-10:00 a.m., 6:30-8:30 p.m.

Bar: Paniolo, 11:00 a.m.-10:30 p.m.

Business Facilities: Audio-visual, Copiers, Telex

Sports Facilities: Tennis courts, Croquet, Putt-putt golf, Riding, Sailing, Snorkeling, Bicycles, Swimming, Fishing, Hula, Scuba diving, Massage

Location: Hana Ranch

Attractions: Museum and cultural center, Waianapanapa State Park, Botanical gardens, Hasegawa General Store

KONA VILLAGE RESORT

Address: P.O. Box 1299, Kaupulehu-Kona 96745
Phone No.: 808-325-5555
Toll-free Cable: 800-367-5290
Telex: 325-6114 KVR
Rates: $$$$*
Credit Cards: AmEx, DC, MC, Visa, CB
No. of Rooms: 100 **Suites:** 25
Services and Amenities: Valet service, Library, Garage and parking, Car hire, Baby-sitting service, Bathroom furnished with 4 sets of thick designer towels, large bars of French milled soap
Restrictions: No pets; portable ramp for handicapped access
Business Facilities: Message center, Audio-visual, Telex
Conference Rooms: 1, capacity 150
Sports Facilities: 3 lighted Laykold tennis courts, croquet, golf course and riding nearby, sailing, snorkeling, outrigger canoes, glass-bottom boat excursions, scuba diving, deep-sea fishing
Location: Secluded area along the Kohala-Kona coast

Remote Kaupulehu is not shown on most maps of "The Big Island." At the foot of Mount Hualalai volcano, isolated by fingers of ancient lava flow, Kona Village is an Eden such as travelers dream about but rarely find.

Guests "live" the Polynesian village experience in individual thatched *hales* beside the white sand beach or the ancient fish pond. These plush/primitive bungalows have no in-room phones, no radios, no TV, but special attention is given to luxurious appointments and special touches like fresh Kona coffee beans, a coffee grinder, and a coffee maker with a wake-up timer.

Renowned interior designer, Mary Philpotts, of Philpotts, Obayashi & Associates, Inc. of Hawaii, has created exotic environments reminiscent of Fiji, Samoa or Tahiti. The Hale Moana dining room is in a New Hebrides-style building overlooking the sea. The blue, green and peach color scheme reflects the natural surroundings. One of the world's largest *tapas*, over 100 feet long, a gift from the Queen of Tonga, hangs in the dining room.

Rates include all meals—and what meals! Is it true that the weekly luau is the very best in the islands? Decide for yourself.

Kona Village Resort is a tribute to founder John Jackson's dream of building a truly timeless Polynesian hideaway where modern people can surround themselves with simplicity and nature. This spot is unique not only in the Hawaiian Islands but in the whole wide world.

IDANHA HOTEL

When the Idanha opened in 1901, it was Boise's grandest hotel. Notable guests included Presidents Theodore Roosevelt and William Taft, and famed lawyers William Jennings Bryan and Clarence Darrow. The Idanha Hotel restoration project has led the way in the city's downtown revitalization, and it has become once more the grandest hotel in the state.

The elegant lobby features marble from Alaska, brass statue lamps and art deco chandeliers. Each of the 70 individually decorated rooms is furnished in an eclectic blend of contemporary and turn-of-the-century styles.

Peter Schott's Continental Restaurant, just off the main lobby, is Boise's finest. The low-key traditional atmosphere is enhanced by Louis XIV chairs, exquisite crystal and white linen tablecloths. Such specialties as gratinee au brie, Belgian endive and radicchio salad Valencia, oysters Christian, poached salmon beurre blanc and a special dessert, Fresh strawberry "Hot Love," keep hotel guests and Boise residents returning time and again.

The hotel's vintage 1948 Packard limousine is available for airport transportation.

Address: 10th & Main St., Boise 83702
Phone No.: 208-342-3611
Rates: $
Credit Cards: Visa, MC, AmEx, DC, Discovery
No. of Rooms: 70 **Suites:** 3
Services and Amenities: Valet service, Parking, Complimentary newspaper, Continental breakfast, TV, Radio
Restrictions: No pets, no handicapped access
Room Service: 7:00 a.m.-10:00 p.m.
Restaurant: Peter Schott's Continental Restaurant, Lunch Mon.-Fri. 11:30 a.m.-2:00 p.m., Dinner Mon.-Sat. 6:00-10:00 p.m.
Bar: Peter Schott's Lounge, 11:30 a.m.-1:00 a.m.
Business Facilities: Available on request
Conference Rooms: 1, capacity 35
Location: Downtown, 15 min. from airport and major highway
Attractions: Historic Boise Tour train (seasonal), Bogus Basin Ski Resort, historical museum, State Capitol, Shakespeare Festival (seasonal)

MAYFAIR REGENT

Address: 181 East Lake Shore Drive, Chicago 60611
Phone No.: 312-787-8500
Reservations: 800-545-4000
Telex: 256266
Rates: $$$*
Credit Cards: AmEx, Visa, MC, DC, CB, JCB
No. of Rooms: 204 **Suites:** 28
Services and Amenities: Gift shop, Laundry, Valet service, Beauty shop, Valet parking, Car hire, International currency exchange, Complimentary shoeshine, House doctor, Baby-sitting service, Complimentary newspaper, TV, Radio, Telephone, Neutrogena soap, Shampoo, Rain bath, Shower Cap, Shoehorn, Shoeshine pad
Restrictions: No pets; no handicapped access
Concierge: 24 hours
Room Service: 24 hours
Restaurant: Ciel Bleu, 7:00 a.m.-10:00 p.m., Dress Code
Business Facilities: Copiers, Telex, Telefax
Conference Rooms: 3, capacity 12-50
Location: Chicago's Gold Coast
Attractions: ½ block from Lake Michigan, fine shopping and restaurant area

On Chicago's Gold Coast overlooking Lake Michigan, this patrician hotel is in the heart of one of Chicago's most prestigious areas, yet just five minutes from downtown. The exquisite lobby features crystal chandeliers, oriental rugs and a Louis XV front desk. The Mayfair Lounge has hand-painted Chinese murals and velvet armchair seating in a color scheme of warm burgundy and beige, a lovely spot for afternoon tea and cocktails accompanied by piano music. Fresh flowers are everywhere, and the ambience is that of an elegant mansion.

The Mayfair Regent emphasizes service—unobtrusive, but constantly at each guest's beck and call. The assistant manager escorts you to your room, and a gracious attendant soon appears to see that everything is in order.

Each guest room contains a large desk and a mini-bar. Furnishings and decor are contemporary, in warm earth tones. The baths have marble vanities, telephones and gigantic bath towels.

On the 19th floor is one of Chicago's finest restaurants, the Ciel Bleu. The lakefront view is beautiful, and the continental cuisine is truly outstanding. A recent fabulous dinner consisted of an hors d'oeuvre of hot goose liver with perigourdine sauce, bisque of scallops with saffron, roast pheasant "Forestier" or veal medallions with morrel sauce, and white chocolate mousse cake with raspberry sauce.

In the event one wishes to work off the feast, guests are extended privileges at the McClurg Court Sports Center.

WHITEHALL

Behind the classic 1920s facade on Chicago's exclusive Gold Coast, you will discover unparalleled comfort, security and privacy with an extraordinarily high staff-to-guest ratio providing most proper service. The lobby's antique panelling is highlighted by an extensive collection of original 19th-Century paintings, and the decor throughout the hotel is that of a fine English country house.
Guest rooms are done in lush green carpeting and peach-hued wall coverings, with furnishings in cherrytone wood and floral chintz fabrics. The baths feature marble vanities, telephones and Rogers & Gallet toiletries. The Hepburn Suite, our favorite, maintains the Old English aura in tones of rich burgundy; it has a full living room, dining area, complete kitchen and balcony.
The Whitehall Club restaurant, in soft muted colors accented by rich wood, bespeaks traditional European elegance. A fabulous dinner here might begin with lobster and crab salad, or the Whitehall salad consisting of bibb lettuce, hearts of palm, avocado, pear and tomato slices; as an entree, perhaps, breast of pheasant with orange sauce; and for dessert, the famed Whitehall chocolate log.
The bar at the Whitehall is a favorite meeting place, whether for an elaborate English high tea or an intimate evening's relaxation to piano and vocal music warmed with the house special, Whitehall coffee.

Address: 105 E. Delaware Place, Chicago 60611
Phone No.: 312-944-6300
Toll-free Cable: 800-621-8295
Telex: 255157
Rates: $$$*
Credit Cards: AmEx, Visa, MC, DC
No. of Rooms: 223 **Suites:** 13
Services and Amenities: Valet service, Garage and parking, Car hire, Complimentary shoeshine, Laundry, House doctor, Baby-sitting service, Currency exchange, Complimentary newspaper, Cable TV, Radio, Bath phone, Robes, Bidet, Bath gel, Shampoo, Hand and body lotion, Glycerine and French milled soaps, Shower cap
Restrictions: No pets; handicapped access to 2 rooms
Concierge: 7:30 a.m.-10:00 p.m.
Room Service: 24 hours
Restaurant: The Whitehall Club, 7:00-11:00 a.m., Noon-2:00 p.m., 6:00-10:00 p.m., Dress Code; The Whitehall Club Bar
Bar: The Bar, Mon.-Fri. 11:00 a.m.-2:00 a.m., Sat.-Sun. 4:00 p.m.-2:00 a.m.
Business Facilities: Secretarial service, Translators, Copiers, Audio-visual, Telex
Sports Facilities: Guests extended privileges to McClurg Court Sports Club
Attractions: Water Tower Place, Oak Street Designer Boutiques, John Hancock Building

TREMONT HOTEL

Address: 100 East Chestnut St., Chicago 60611
Phone No.: 312-751-1900
Toll-free Cable: 800-621-8133
Telex: 255157
Rates: $$$*
Credit Cards: AmEx, Visa, MC, DC
No. of Rooms: 139 **Suites:** 9
Services and Amenities: Valet service, Laundry, Garage and parking, Car hire, Complimentary shoeshine, House doctor, Babysitting service, Complimentary newspaper, Cable TV, Phone in bath, Bath gel, Shampoo, Body lotion, Glycerine soap, Milled soap, Shower cap
Restrictions: No pets; handicapped access to 1 room
Concierge: 10:00 a.m.-6:00 p.m.
Room Service: 24 hours
Restaurant: Cricket's, 7:00-11:00 a.m., Noon-2:30 p.m., 6:00-10:30 p.m., Dress Code
Bar: Cricket's Hearth, Noon-1:00 a.m.
Business Facilities: Translators, Copiers, Audio-visual, Telex
Conference Rooms: 4, capacity 10-140
Attractions: Shopping, Boutiques, Water Tower Place, Taste of Chicago, International Art Fair, Gold Coast Art Fair

The Tremont Hotel offers discerning travelers the warm, inviting ambience of an English manor, superbly located on Chicago's elite Gold Coast. Flawless service satisfies each guest's wishes in a most private atmosphere.

The rooms are spacious and beautifully decorated with Clarence House fabrics in tones of green, orange and beige. The elegant furnishings include oriental chests and writing desks, and the sumptuous baths contain every amenity one could desire. A favorite suite, The Wicker, has dark tile floors and wicker furniture with brightly colored pillows. The panoramic city views from this suite are stunning!

Cricket's Hearth restaurant is among Chicago's finest. The lighthearted spirit here is reflected in its artwork, table linens, leather banquettes and wood plank floor. For dinner you may enjoy shrimp sautee vin blanc, followed by fresh Dover sole Veronique or tournedos saute aux deux poivres, served with au gratin potatoes and endive and beef vinaigrette; and for dessert, Grand Marnier souffle with sauce au chocolat.

The atmosphere in Cricket's Bar is one of conviviality. The race horse theme appears in engravings and antique horse and jockey figures. Try a Cricket's coffee, the house special, while enjoying the live entertainment.

Guests are extended privileges to the McClurg Court Sports Center.

DE SOTO HOUSE

A legend has returned to life in Galena, one of the upper Midwest's favorite historic districts. First opened in 1855, the De Soto House was known as "the best hotel west of New York City." A variety of famous visitors, including Abraham Lincoln, established the hotel's world-wide reputation in that era of grace and elegance.

De Soto House was renovated in 1985 beyond even its original splendor, and all modern conveniences were added. The lobby, with its original molded tin ceilings and semi-circular grand carved stairway, is a joy to behold.

Each of the 55 large guest rooms is individually decorated in high Victorian style with floral wall papers, luxury fabrics and an armoire within which the TV is concealed.

Truffles, the romantic restaurant, has country French decor in a color scheme of burgundy and rose—and the food is sensational. A few of the delights available are coquille cardinal, caviar beluga malossal, salad parmachee, chateaubriand Cecilia, and as a final fillip, Souffle Grand Marnier. Truffles also has an intimate piano bar.

Galena hosts many special country fairs and festivals, and is known for its fine antique shops. Other local activities include year-round sports and Mississippi River paddleboat tours.

Address: 230 South Main St., Galena 61036
Phone No.: 815-777-0090
Toll-free Cable: 800-233-3905
Rates: $
Credit Cards: AmEx, Visa, MC, DC, CB
No. of Rooms: 55 **Suites:** 2
Services and Amenities: Laundry, Valet service, Garage and parking, Complimentary shoeshine, Baby-sitting service, Gift shop, Cable TV, VCR available, Telephone
Restrictions: No pets; handicapped access to 5 rooms
Room Service: 24 hours
Restaurant: Truffles, 7:00 a.m.-10:00 p.m.; The Grand Court
Bar: Truffles, 11:00 a.m.-1:00 a.m.
Business Facilities: Message center, Secretarial service, Translators, Copiers, Audio-visual
Conference Rooms: 5, 5700 square feet
Location: Downtown Galena
Attractions: Antique shops, historic Galena, near river boat rides, greyhound racetrack

BOURBON ORLEANS HOTEL

Address: 717 Orleans St., New Orleans 70116
Phone No.: 504-523-2222
Toll-free Cable: 800-521-5338
Telex: 510101085
Rates: $$*
Credit Cards: AmEx, Visa, MC, DC
No. of Rooms: 211 **Suites:** 49
Services and Amenities: Laundry, Valet service, Valet parking, Complimentary shoeshine, Complimentary newspaper, TV, Radio, Telephone, Robes, TV in each bathroom, Shampoo, Bath gel, Soap
Restrictions: No pets; no handicapped access
Concierge: 9:00 a.m.-5:00 p.m.
Room Service: 24 hours
Restaurant: Lafayette's, 7:00 a.m.-11:00 p.m.
Bar: Promenade, 10:00 a.m.-1:00 a.m.
Business Facilities: Message center, Secretarial service, Copiers, Audio-visual, Teleconferencing, Telex, Complete business center
Conference Rooms: 5, capacity 500
Location: French Quarter
Attractions: Walking distance to Jackson Square with famous St. Louis Cathedral, Prebytere Museum and French Market

When the New Orleans Ballroom opened in 1817, it rivaled the glittering salons of Europe. Newly restored, the ballroom has become the centerpiece of one of the finest hotels on the Vieux Carre (French Quarter). The lobby has lofty ceilings, tall classic columns, wingback chairs and loveseats.

The guest rooms maintain the 19th-Century French Country style with Queen Anne and Chippendale furniture, rich floor-length curtains and poster or half-canopied beds. The oversized marble baths feature TV, telephone, bath sheets, robes and a full complement of toiletries. Nightly turn-down service comes complete with a goodnight mint on the pillow.

The hotel restaurant, the Lafayette, is elegantly appointed with peach linen tablecloths, Villeroy and Boch china and etched glassware. Dinner might begin with an hors d'oeuvre of chicken, pears and walnuts, continue with shrimp Samuels or a carpetbagger steak with oyster stuffing; and finish with a Bourbon Street tart.

The Promenade Bar is a favorite gathering place. The old-fashioned antique bar serves up a mint julep straight from the original Old South recipe.

French Quarter charm and elegance are pervasive, from the wrought iron railings and tranquil inner courtyard to the massive white-columned facade that frames the main entrance on Orleans Street. Jackson Square, St. Louis Cathedral and the French Market are only steps away.

PONTCHARTRAIN HOTEL

The Pontchartrain Hotel, centrally located in the Garden District, was built in 1927 by the Aschaffenburg family, who still own and manage the property. The magnificent draped entrance opens into a grand lobby with vaulted ceiling and gleaming chandeliers.

Each spacious guest room is individually decorated, no two alike. The suites in this hotel are truly extraordinary. For example, the Richard Burton suite is decorated on a "Camelot" theme in honor of the late, great actor; and the magnificent new Imperial suite has Napoleonic decor in the Malmaison tradition.

For elegant dining atmosphere, the Caribbean Room is done in gorgeous shades of rose and pink and features wall murals by Charles Reinike. The cuisine, meticulously prepared, presents a tantalizing blend of French and Creole flavors. Oyster broth sets the stage for crabmeat Remick, tenderloin of beef Marchand, heart of artichoke Clamart, cheese and fruit a la Maison, all crowned by Mile-High pie. The excellent wine list offers both European and American vintages.

The Bayou Bar was inspired by the natural beauty of Louisiana scenic backwaters, again reflected in a Reinike wall mural. Piano music adds to your enjoyment of house specialties such as the mint julep and the Bayou Bomb.

Guests are extended privileges to Racquet Ball One, a full spa and health club.

50 years of one-family ownership make for conscientious quality service that is unrivaled anywhere.

Address: 2031 St. Charles Avenue, New Orleans 70140
Phone No.: 504-524-0581
Toll-free Cable: 800-952-8092
Telex: 266068 PONT
Reservation Services: Robert F. Warner at Preferred Hotels
Rates: $$*
Credit Cards: All major credit cards
No. of Rooms: 100 **Suites:** 28
Services and Amenities: Valet service, Laundry, House doctor, Baby-sitting service, Garage and parking, Complimentary newspaper, Cable TV, Shampoo, Soap, Conditioners, Vitabath, Radio
Restrictions: No pets; no handicapped access
Concierge: Front desk, 7:00 a.m.-11:00 p.m.
Room Service: 7:00 a.m.-11:00 p.m.
Restaurant: Caribbean Room, 11:45 a.m.-2:00 p.m., 6:00-10:00 p.m.; Cafe Pontchartrain, 7:00 8:30 a.m., 11:00 a.m.-4:00 p.m., 5:00-8:30 p.m.; Dress Code
Bar: Bayou Bar, Mon.-Thur. 10:00 a.m.-1:00 a.m., Fri.-Sat. 10:00 a.m.-2:00 a.m.
Business Facilities: Telex, Audio-visual rental
Conference Rooms: 3, capacity 40
Attractions: Mississippi River cruises, French Quarter, Garden District, antique shopping

BETHEL INN

Address: P.O. Box 49, Bethel 04217
Phone No.: 207-824-2175
Rates: $
Credit Cards: AmEx, DC, MC, Visa, CB
No. of Rooms: 70 **Suites:** 8
Services and Amenities: Gift shop, Library, Garage and parking, Baby-sitting service, Laundry, Direct-dial telephone, Shampoo, Soap, Lotion, Large towels
Restrictions: Pets by prior arrangement; handicapped access to 2 rooms
Concierge: Mid-morning-mid-afternoon
Room Service: Breakfast only, 7:30-9:00 a.m.
Restaurant: Main and South Dining Room, 7:30 a.m.-9:00 a.m., Noon-2:00 p.m., 6:00 p.m.-9:00 p.m.
Bar: Millbrook Tavern, Noon-1:00 a.m.
Business Facilities: Complete business center, Message center, Secretarial service, Copiers, Audio-visual, Teleconferencing
Conference Rooms: 9, capacity 275
Sports Facilities: Hard-surface tennis court, handball/squash, croquet, 9-hole golf course, sailing, lake & pool swimming, cross-country skiing on property
Location: Village Common
Attractions: Local pottery, Shaker furniture maker, rustic antiques, covered bridges, waterfalls, caves, hiking trails

Bethel Inn is a cluster of five Colonial mansion-style guest buildings and a lake house, some dating back to 1850, on 85 rolling acres of lovely gardens and shaded paths. All guest rooms are within a hundred yards of the main building fronting on the Village Common in Bethel's National Historic District. Seventy miles from Portland, Maine, the Inn is fully equipped as both a resort and a state of the art conference center.

Guest rooms are Colonial American in decor. The comfortably old-fashioned bathrooms feature spacious tubs, large towels, direct dial telephones and ample amenities. A corner suite in the Oaks Building has a cozy bedroom and a large sitting room with fireplace and adjoining veranda.

The two dining rooms are country elegant, aglow with sunlight, with views of the golf course. Some favorite dishes are asparagus tips wrapped in ham, veal Oscar, and lemon icebox cake.

The rustic barn board Millbrook Tavern offers seasonal house specialties: hot Schonopolate in winter, fresh frozen daiquiris in summer. Tables are often moved back to make room for dancing to live entertainment.

In the summer and fall, guests enjoy afternoon tea served in the Gibson room to the strains of classical music performances.

The Bethel Inn is also a complete country club with a 9-hole golf course, swimming, croquet, tennis courts and sailing. There is a sauna to warm you up after skiing—two downhill slopes just ten minutes away, or cross-country from the Inn's back door.

BLACK POINT INN

Rugged cliffs, wide sandy beaches and fragrant pine and balsam woods surround the Black Point Inn, a fine traditional resort on a secluded peninsula. The architecture is "Down East," the atmosphere one of unpretentious elegance—a retreat recalling the calm of a former time in a setting of timeless beauty.

The guest room decor radiates New England charm with white crewel bedspreads, ruffled priscilla curtains, rock maple furnishings and delicate print wall paper. All baths have been newly remodelled and appointed with towels, robes and complimentary toiletries.

Sporting facilities include 14 tennis courts, a PGA-rated 18-hole golf course, two pools—indoor and outdoor—and a whirlpool and sauna. Guests are extended privileges at the Prout's Neck Country Club and the Prout's Neck Yacht Club.

The dining room has a lovely ocean view. The water-stained pine woodwork and Victorian wall paper continue the aura of New England at its finest. The most celebrated entree is fresh, succulent Maine lobster. A delicious dinner may include liver pate with truffles; raspberry soup chambord; baked native scallops au beurre or roast stuffed Long Island duckling; and a classic hot apple pie with cheese or locally made ice cream.

A haven of tradition, the Black Point Inn serves tea and cookies daily during the July-August social season. The popular "Meeting Room" has a dance floor where a musical trio or quartet plays on weekends.

Outstanding conference facilities invite executives to select the inn as a corporate meeting site, and the location—only ten miles from Portland International Jetport—makes access easy.

Address: Route 207, Prout's Neck 04074
Phone No.: 207-883-4126
Rates: $$$
Credit Cards: Visa, MC
No. of Rooms: 80 **Suites:** 4
Services and Amenities: Gift shop, Valet service, Library, Barber shop, Beauty shop, Garage and parking, Baby-sitting service with advance notice, Laundry, Telephone, Robes, Shampoo, Conditioners, Milled soaps, Sewing kits, Shower caps, Shoeshine
Restrictions: No pets; no handicapped access; No children under 5 during July-August
Concierge: 7:00 a.m.-5:00 p.m.
Room Service: Yes
Restaurant: Dining Room, 8:00-9:30 a.m., 12:30-2:00 p.m., 7:00-8:30 p.m., Dress Code
Bar: The Meeting Room, 5:00 p.m.-Midnight
Business Facilities: Copiers, Audio-visual, Teleconferencing, Translators on request
Conference Rooms: 3, capacity 200
Sports Facilities: 14 clay & asphalt tennis courts, 18-hole PGA-rated golf course, sailing, 2 swimming pools
Location: On the ocean
Attractions: Bird sanctuary, cliff walk, cottage of Winslow Homer

PEABODY COURT

Address: 612 Cathedral St., Baltimore 21201
Phone No.: 301-727-7101
Toll-free Cable: 800-732-5301
Telex: 292126
Reservation Services: 800-223-6800
Rates: $$*
Credit Cards: AmEx, MC, Visa, DC, CB, CH
No. of Rooms: 104 **Suites:** 25
Services and Amenities: Valet service, Library, Garage and parking, Car hire, Currency exchange, Laundry, Complimentary shoeshine, Baby-sitting service, Complimentary newspaper, Cable TV, Radio, Wet bar, Jacuzzi, Towel warmer, Bath phone
Restrictions: $20 charge for pets; handicapped access to 5 rooms
Concierge: 24 hours
Room Service: 24 hours
Restaurant: The Conservatory, La Brasserie, Dress Code
Bar: Conservatory Lounge
Business Facilities: Complete business service center, arrangements made through concierge
Conference Rooms: 8, capacity 250
Sports Facilities: Guest privileges at Downtown Athletic Club
Location: Mt. Vernon Place, Downtown Baltimore
Attractions: Historic Baltimore, theatres, galleries, Inner Harbor

This 1930 neo-classical structure, certified as a National Historic Site, was totally renovated and re-opened in 1985 as a truly world-class hotel. From the palatial lobby with its six-foot Baccarat chandelier, to the 105 guest rooms furnished in Directoire period decor, extraordinary attention to quality and luxury is visible in every detail.

Rooms are large, comfortable and handsomely appointed with fine fabrics and superb furnishings imported from Italy. The bathrooms feature Italian marble, towel-warming racks, sun lamps and Jacuzzis.

Opulence pervades the two dining rooms. La Brasserie, on the second floor, serves informal breakfast, lunch and dinner. The Conservatory, atop the hotel on the 14th story, is decorated in lavish Belle Epoch style and affords a breathtaking view of Baltimore. In the lounge, as if splendor alone were not enough, the bar frames Joseph Shepard's impressive mural, "The Judgment of Paris."

The food, too, is exceptionally fine. Chef Michel Laudier has created a cuisine to rival the finest in Europe.

TIDEWATER INN

Here is an intimate inn to which guests return year after year. The handsome four-story structure, Federal in design, is the pride of Easton's National Historic District. Strolling the village or relaxing by the fire in the homey parlor, you will feel as if you've slipped back into Colonial days.

The aura of history come to life pervades the Inn's public areas and guest rooms. The comfortably elegant decor is highlighted by fine wood panelling, richly upholstered furniture and antique appointments throughout.

The location on Maryland's fabled Eastern Shore makes the Inn a popular retreat among sportsmen who come for the regattas and the legendary fishing. For others, a favorite pastime is the village's incomparable antique shopping.

The Crystal Room's elegant formal decor sets the stage for fabulous Chesapeake cuisine. Home-cooked Maryland crab cakes, crab Norfolk or soft-shelled crabs are a seafood lover's delight.

From Baltimore, Washington D.C. or Philadelphia, the Tidewater Inn is only a few hours' drive—and, in spirit, two centuries distant.

Address: Dover & Harrison St., Easton 21601
Phone No.: 301-822-1300
Rates: $
Credit Cards: AmEx, DC, MC, Visa, Choice
No. of Rooms: 119 **Suites:** 6
Services and Amenities: Gift shop, Valet service, Parking, Laundry, House doctor, Phone, TV
Restrictions: Handicapped access to 2 rooms
Room Service: 7:00 a.m.-10:00 p.m.
Restaurant: Crystal Room and River Room, 7:00 a.m.-10:00 p.m., Dress Code
Bar: Decoy Bar, 11:00 a.m.-2:00 p.m.
Business Facilities: Message center, Copiers, Audio-visual, Other services upon request
Conference Rooms: 8, capacity 40-300
Sports Facilities: Golf courses, charter fishing, access to health spa
Location: Historic downtown near Rt. 50
Attractions: Chesapeake Bay

THE RITZ-CARLTON

Address: 15 Arlington St., Boston 02117
Phone No.: 617-536-5700
Toll-free Cable: 800-241-3333
Telex: 940591
Rates: $$$*
Credit Cards: All major credit cards and Ritz-Carlton card
No. of Rooms: 279 **Suites:** 41
Services and Amenities: Valet service, Barber shop, Garage and parking, Currency exchange, Complimentary shoeshine, Baby-sitting service, Laundry, Gift shop, Complimentary newspaper, TV, Clock-radio, Hair dryers, Robes
Restrictions: Pets on leash by prior arrangement; handicapped access to 8 rooms
Concierge: 24 hours
Room Service: 24 hours
Restaurant: Dining Room, Noon-2:30 p.m., 6:00-11:00 p.m., Dress Code
Bar: Ritz Bar, Mon.-Sat. 11:30 a.m.-1:00 a.m., Sun. 4:00 p.m.-Midnight
Business Facilities: Secretarial service, Copiers, Telex
Conference Rooms: 13, capacity 500
Sports Facilities: Health club, sauna, massage, weight training
Location: Downtown Back Bay, limo transport from airport, Arlington stop on public transport
Attractions: Boston Public Garden

For more than half a century, gracious service and time-honored elegance have combined to make the Ritz-Carlton a Bostonian tradition. From its magnificent grand ballroom, to its exclusive Back Bay location, to its highly professional 400-person staff, this hotel sets the standard by which excellence is measured.

Attention to detail shows in the gold service, genuine Irish linen, hand polished brass, white-gloved elevator operators, and fresh flowers everywhere. On weekdays, the hotel provides complimentary chauffeured limousine service to guests with appointments in the financial district or other areas of the city.

The large guest rooms are furnished in classic French provincial style accented with imported fabrics and distinctive works of art. Fluffy robes hang in baths of Vermont marble with porcelain fixtures and oversized tubs. The Presidential Suite on the 7th floor has full-height windows overlooking historic Beacon Hill.

A delightful meal in the main dining room, with its expansive view of Boston's Public Garden, might begin with caviar, followed by poached salmon with lobster sauce, then a pear sorbet; as an entree, rack of lamb with vegetables; and for a sweet conclusion, a sky-high chocolate souffle. The wine cellar contains 10,000 bottles—you will undoubtedly find one you like.

Tea is served daily in the Lounge, and after-dinner cigars and cognac are a nightly ritual. The clublike Ritz Bar, with its glowing fireplace and rich warm panelling, is a Boston favorite. Be sure to try the famous (and delightful) "Ritz Fizz."

FOUR SEASONS

Boston's lovely Four Seasons Hotel, newly opened in June 1985, has already earned its place in the pantheon of great small hotels thanks to its intimate feel, exquisite view and European quality service.

The decor is a mellow blend of Old World charm, elegant Bostonian simplicity and modern architectural styling. Guest rooms are large and exceptionally well appointed. Several non-smokers' rooms are available. Among the hotel's best features are expansive windows on all floors commanding spectacular views of the famed Public Garden across the street.

The Bristol Lounge at the foot of the grand staircase is open daily for breakfast, lunch, afternoon tea, dinner and late-night repasts. You may enjoy cocktails and hors d'oeuvres to the accompaniment of piano music in the lounge. For a more complete meal, the restaurant Aujourd'hui provides traditionally elegant service. The international wine list changes daily to complement the menu. *Table d'hote* is available for lunch and dinner, as well as a full *a la carte* menu in the classic French manner; and an innovative alternate menu features gourmet dishes with reduced calories, sodium and cholesterol. A hint to dining connoisseurs: try one of the special souffles.

The exclusive Beacon Hill location affords convenient access to the best of everything in the city. Nearby are Faneuil Hall marketplace, Newberry Street's world-famous boutiques and art galleries, and all major cultural activities.

Address: 200 Boylston Street, Boston 02116
Phone No.: 617-338-4400
Toll-free Cable: US 800-828-1188, Canada 800-268-6282
Telex: 853349
Rates: $$$*
Credit Cards: All major credit cards
No. of Rooms: 288 **Suites:** 13
Services and Amenities: Valet service, Garage and parking, Car hire, Currency exchange, Laundry, Complimentary shoeshine, House doctor, Baby-sitting service, Complimentary newspaper, Cable TV, Phone in bath, Robes, Shampoo, Special soaps, Gel
Restrictions: Small pets; handicapped access to 16 rooms
Concierge: 24 hours
Room Service: 24 hours
Restaurant: Aujourd'hui, 7:00 a.m.-10:30 p.m., Dress Code
Bar: Bristol Lounge, 11:30 a.m.-1:30 a.m.
Business Facilities: Copiers, Audio-visual, Telex, Additional business services arranged through concierge
Conference Rooms: 7
Sports Facilities: Full health spa, Swimming pool, Whirlpool, Sauna, Massage, Weight room, Aerobics area available
Attractions: Copley Place, Newbury Street antique shops

HARBOR VIEW HOTEL

Address: North Water Street, Edgartown 02539
Phone No.: 617-627-4333
Toll-free Cable: 800-225-6005 (Northeast except Mass.)
Rates: $$$
Credit Cards: AmEx, MC, Visa
No. of Rooms: 127 **Suites:** 22
Services and Amenities: Garage and parking, Baby-sitting service, Card/game area, TV, Bidet, Telephone
Restrictions: No pets; handicapped access to 1 room
Room Service: During meal hours
Restaurant: Starbuck's, 8:00-10:00 a.m., 12:00-3:00 p.m., 6:00-9:00 p.m.
Bar: Starbuck's, Noon-Midnight
Business Facilities: Copiers, Audio-visual
Conference Rooms: 4, capacity 200
Sports Facilities: 2 tennis courts, swimming pool, golf, riding, sailing nearby
Location: ⅓ mi. from downtown Edgartown in resort area
Attractions: On Edgartown Harbor, beach, near downtown shops

The Harbor View Hotel, as its name suggests, commands a spectacular view of Nantucket Sound. Built in 1891 in New England Victorian style, the hotel has recently been refurbished throughout. The 127 rooms, 22 of which are suites, share a style bespeaking casual elegance. The rooms are quite large, and many have balconies overlooking the harbor. Baths are also spacious and have telephones.

Starbuck's, the famous Edgartown "watering hole," serves New England and continental cuisine in relaxed surroundings. A recent wonderful dinner consisted of their Littleneck clam bar, Tournedos Rossini, and Strawberry cheesecake for dessert Music and dancing enliven the atmosphere later in the evening.

The fabulous beachfront location invites romantic strolls on the sand. There are also a swimming pool and two all-weather tennis courts, and golf, riding, sailing and antique shopping are close by. In summary, the Harbor View is a delightful small resort in the heart of one of New England's most popular vacation areas.

KELLEY HOUSE

This inn's harborside location in the heart of town lends itself admirably to an intimate Edgartown experience. With only 60 rooms, ample attention is paid to each guest's needs.

The rooms, furnished and wallpapered in authentic Colonial style, match the setting perfectly. A favorite suite has a cathedral ceiling, a large living room and a patio with a view of the harbor.

The restaurant, Zachariah's, is noted for its casual ambience and seafood menu. An extravaganza of specialties such as stuffed sole in puff pastry with scallops and shrimp in Newburg sauce, steamed mussels with basil, and baked stuffed lobster will please the most discerning palate. For meat lovers, the veal Czarina is outstanding; and everybody adores the Toll House pie.

Guests tend to congregate by the outdoor pool where cocktails are served from noon to 6 p.m.

From the central location, all the activities of this renowned area await your pleasure.

Address: One Kelley Street, Edgartown 02539
Phone No.: 617-627-4394
Rates: $$*
Credit Cards: Visa, MC, AmEx
No. of Rooms: 60 **Suites:** 6
Townhouses: 2
Services and Amenities: Valet service, Garage and parking, Complimentary newspaper, TV, Telephone, Bidet, Complimentary toiletries
Restrictions: No pets; no handicapped access
Restaurant: Zachariah's, 7:30-10:00 a.m., 12:00-2:00 p.m., 6:00-9:00 p.m.
Bar: Service bar in restaurant; poolside cocktails
Business Facilities: Front desk message center, Audio-visual
Conference Rooms: 1, capacity 60
Sports Facilities: 2 tennis courts, swimming pool
Location: Center of Edgartown, near harbor
Attractions: Edgartown shopping, sports nearby, island tours

DEARBORN INN

Address: 20301 Oakwood Boulevard, Dearborn 48124
Phone No.: 313-271-2700
Toll-free Cable: 800-221-7236 US, 800-221-7237 MI
Rates: $
Credit Cards: AmEx, MC, Visa, DC, CB
No. of Rooms: 179 **Suites:** 6
Services and Amenities: Gift shop, Valet service, Baby-sitting service, Laundry, TV and Radio, Telephone, Shampoo, Shower cap, Hand and body lotion, Bath and shower gel, Lint brush, Soap
Restrictions: Pets in Colonial Homes and Motor House, cannot be left in room alone; no handicapped access
Room Service: 6:00 a.m.-12:00 p.m.
Restaurant: Early American Room, Mon.-Fri. 11:15 a.m.-1:30 p.m., 6:00 p.m.-10:00 p.m., Sat. 6:00 p.m.-11:00 p.m., Sun. brunch 10:00 a.m.-2:00 p.m.; Ten Eyck Tavern 6:30 a.m.-10:00 p.m. daily
Bar: Golden Eagle Lounge, Mon.-Fri. 11:30 a.m.-1:00 a.m., Sat. 4:30 p.m.-1:00 a.m., prime rib buffet Mon.-Fri. 11:30 a.m.-2:00 p.m.
Business Facilities: Copiers, Audio-visual
Conference Rooms: 7
Sports Facilities: 2 tennis courts, AAU size pool
Location: Suburban
Attractions: 5 min. from Fairlane Town Center shopping mall, across the street from Greenfield Village and Henry Ford Museum, 30 min. from Canada via Ambassador Bridge or Tunnel

Henry Ford built the Dearborn Inn in 1931 as a convenience for early travelers to the area. Mr. Ford's admiration for Georgian architecture is readily apparent. The lobby, with its muted colors and early American furniture, has a warm homelike atmosphere. Of the 179 rooms, 94 are in the Inn itself, while the others are located in separate buildings on the property, five of them reproductions of the homes of famous Americans. The theme of early American reproduction furniture and Georgian sensibility is carried throughout the guest rooms.

The cuisine offered in the 2 dining rooms is All-American, with such specialties as Michigan bean soup, whitefish from the Great Lakes, and prime rib. For dessert, what else but apple pie? The Friday seafood buffet is a Michigan tradition.

Guests are extended privileges at the Fairlane Club, and there is ed pool on the premises for seasonal use. The 23 beautifully landscaped acres provide a quiet locale for conferences.

Directly across from the Inn, Greenfield Village and Henry Ford Museum feature the world's largest indoor-outdoor collection of Americana . . .Truly fascinating.

OMNI INTERNATIONAL

This ultra-modern hotel, with its spectacular seven-story glass atrium, is in Millender Center, connected by a second-floor walkway to the Renaissance Center. The shopping and entertainment complex in the heart of downtown Detroit is regarded by many as the prototype for 21st-Century cities, and the Omni fits right in.

Each oversized guest room is decorated in a blue or green color scheme with polished cherry furnishings and many special touches. Bathrooms have marble vanities, extra large tubs, telephones, huge towels and complimentary toiletries. The suites, even bigger, are ideal for small meetings or entertaining.

333 East—the restaurant, that is—features a greenhouse area lush with exotic plants, a welcome haven from the northern winter. Furnished in contemporary style and richly decorated in rose, blue and green hues, this is a delightful spot in which to savor excellent cuisine. To begin, why not try a California chevre in puff pastry, served with caramelized currant sauce? Next, perhaps a salad of American field greens with sage dressing, and an entree of grilled Pacific salmon. Chocolate ganache torte and a cup of Jamaican Blue Mountain coffee conclude the meal perfectly.

A complete health club on the premises offers Nautilus exercise equipment, tennis, racquet ball, indoor pool, whirlpool, steam room and jogging track.

Omni International Hotel
Address: 333 East Jefferson St., Detroit 48226
Phone No.: 313-222-7700
Toll-free Cable: 800-THE-OMNI
Rates: $$*
Credit Cards: AmEx, MC, Visa, DC, CB
No. of Rooms: 258 **Suites:** 18
Services and Amenities: Gift shop, Valet service, Barber shop, Garage and parking, Car hire, International currency exchange, Laundry, Complimentary shoeshine, Complimentary newspaper, Baby-sitting service, Cable TV, Radio, Telephones, Robes, Complimentary toiletries
Restrictions: No pets; handicapped access to 13 rooms
Concierge: 7:00 a.m.-11:00 p.m.
Room Service: 24 hours
Restaurant: 333 East, 6:00 a.m.-10:00 p.m., Fri.-Sat. 6:00 a.m.-11:00 p.m.
Bar: Lobby Bar, 11:00 a.m.-2:00 a.m., Sun. Noon-Midnight
Business Facilities: Secretarial service, Copiers, Audio-visual, Telex
Conference Rooms: 4, 800 square feet each, and 3 executive meeting rooms
Sports Facilities: 2 outdoor tennis courts, handball/squash, swimming, full health spa, whirlpool, sauna, massage, aerobics, weight training
Location: Downtown
Attractions: Greenfield Village, Greektown, Detroit Institute of the Arts, Detroit Zoo, Joe Louis Arena, Ford Auditorium, Windsor, Canada

THE SAINT PAUL

Address: 350 Market Street, St. Paul 55102
Phone No.: 612-292-9292
Toll-free Cable: 800-457-9292
Reservation Services: Princess/Lowes, 212-715-7024, 212-841-1687
Rates: $
Credit Cards: Visa, MC, AmEx, CB, DC
No. of Rooms: 254 **Suites:** 30
Services and Amenities: Gift shop, Valet service, Garage and valet parking, Laundry, Car hire, International currency exchange, Baby-sitting service, Cable TV, Radio, Shampoo, Rinse, Soap, Shower cap
Restrictions: No pets; handicapped access to 12 rooms
Concierge: Variable hours, 10:00 a.m.-10:00 p.m.
Room Service: 6:30 a.m.-11:00 p.m.
Restaurant: L'Etoile, 11:30 a.m.-2:30 p.m., 6:00-11:00 p.m., Dress Code; The Cafe, 6:00 a.m.-10:00 a.m.
Bar: The Bar, 3:00 p.m.-1:00 a.m.
Business Facilities: Message center, Secretarial service, Copiers, Audio-visual, Teleconferencing, Telex
Conference Rooms: 7, capacity 965
Location: Rice Park with limousine service to airport and ½ mile from major highway
Attractions: Canterbury Downs Race Track, 45 min.; Paddle-wheel river boat on Mississippi; In heart of theatre district & downtown shopping

This 1910 Twin Cities grand hotel has been elegantly reborn. In the heart of downtown St. Paul, overlooking Rice Park, the building is mirrored in the reflective windows of surrounding modern skyscrapers to appear twice its actual size. Since restoration its rooms are fewer but more spacious, and the intimate Old World charm provides a splendid setting for business or pleasure.

Four crystal chandeliers in the lobby lounge sparkle on mirrored tabletops, amid rich red furnishings, oriental-design carpeting and massive stone columns. The aura is one of ultimate peace and quiet, privacy and security.

Spacious guest rooms emphasize comfort, with traditional decor and a beige or green color scheme. Many rooms offer outstanding views of the park below, and all have cable TV. Each bath has a basket overflowing with delightful toiletries.

The continental L'Etoile is one of Saint Paul's finest restaurants. Baked oyster L'Etoile and Minnesota wild rice soup set the stage for the contra filet of lamb Paul Bocuse, and you may complete your meal with a chocolate schaume torte.

Catered affairs are a specialty at the Saint Paul. From small informal parties *en suite* to grand balls, the highly professional staff can help make any event truly special.

The city's downtown Skyway—the world's largest network of all-weather indoor walkways—connects the hotel with St. Paul's shopping, government and financial districts as well as theatres, libraries and museums.

WENTWORTH HOTEL

An old stone bridge over the Wildcat River leads from quaint Jackson village (population 600) to Wentworth Resort Hotel. Built in 1869, Wentworth Hall was among the many New England grand resorts that catered to affluent 19th Century society. While most such "golden era" getaways have long since vanished, Wentworth has recently been renovated to provide an authentic escape back into that opulent era.

Open year-round, Wentworth Resort Hotel now offers full modern business conference facilities for up to 75 people, while maintaining traditional standards of quality and service.

The guest rooms feature blonde French provincial furniture and relaxing pastel color schemes. Many of the well-appointed baths have antique claw-footed tubs.

The restaurant, The Plum Room, is also done in blonde French provincial, with plum, pink and mauve colors. Tables are set in fine gold-rimmed Jackson china and pink crystal, with fresh flowers on each table. We recommend the seafood melange, followed by the popular Wentworth scampi, and perhaps pecan pie for dessert.

Recreation on the property includes an 18-hole PGA golf course, a clay tennis court and a 140 kilometer ski trail that begins right at the doorstep. The resort is surrounded by the 1,200-square-mile White Mountain National Forest, with 86 mountains and several downhill ski slopes nearby.

The village has a number of fine shops and galleries for browsing. Seasonal events include the Arts Jubilee, Winterfest, and the equestrian classic, "Jumping in the Clouds."

Wentworth Hotel and Resort
Address: P.O. Box M, Jackson 03846
Phone No.: 603-383-9700
Reservation Service: Chamber of Commerce, 603-356-3171
Rates: $
Credit Cards: AmEx, MC, Visa
No. of Rooms: 65 **Suites:** 6
Services and Amenities: Library, Baby-sitting service, Laundry, Cable TV, 2 different soaps
Restrictions: No pets; no highchairs or cribs; no handicapped access
Concierge: Summer-fall, variable hours
Room Service: Limited-variable hours
Restaurant: Plum Room, 8:00-10:00 a.m., 6:00-10:00 p.m.; Clubhouse, Noon-9:00 p.m.
Bar: Wentworth Lounge, 4:00 p.m.-1:00 a.m.
Business Facilities: Message center, Secretarial service, Copiers, Audio-visual rental available
Conference Rooms: 2, capacity 75 and 15-20
Sports Facilities: Clay tennis court, 18-hole golf course
Location: Village Center
Attractions: Factory outlets, Storyland, Mt. Washington, Arts Jubilee, Winterfest

HANOVER INN

Address: East Wheelock & Main Street, P.O. Box 151, Hanover 03755
Phone No.: 603-643-4300
Rates: $
Credit Cards: AmEx, Visa, MC, DC
No. of Rooms: 101 **Suites:** 6
Services and Amenities: Clothier shop, Valet service, Garage and parking, Baby-sitting service, Laundry, Cable TV, Radio, Telephone, Robes, Complimentary toiletries
Restrictions: Small pets; no handicapped access
Room Service: 8:00-10:00 a.m.
Restaurant: Daniel Webster Room, Ivy Grill, breakfast, lunch and dinner, Dress Code
Bar: Ivy Grill, 11:00 a.m.-Midnight
Business Facilities: Copiers, Audio-visual
Conference Rooms: 8, capacity 300
Sports Facilities: Access to Dartmouth sports facilities, guest privileges to Hanover Country Club
Location: Dartmouth College Campus
Attractions: Museums, shopping, Quechee Gorge, Dartmouth College

On the edge of Dartmouth College campus, guests at Hanover Inn enjoy access to all of the school's athletic facilities as well as its art exhibits, plays, concerts and films.

The architecture is Georgian brick, and the environs are those of a small New England village. Colonial styling in shades of beige accented with rose and green is featured throughout the inn, and each guest room is individually decorated. Baths have telephones, robes and ample deluxe personal care amenities.

The Daniel Webster Room serves classic American fare in an atmosphere of Edwardian elegance. The Ivy Grill, with its upbeat contemporary ambience, serves American cuisine and offers an extensive and unique appetizer list. Afternoon high tea is served Monday through Friday in the Hayward Lounge, which is appointed like a fine living room. Included are a wide assortment of pastries made on the premises.

The surrounding Upper Connecticut River Valley, one of America's most scenic areas, provides ample opportunities for picnicking, hiking, swimming, fishing and skiing.

Intended as lodgings for visiting parents and alumni, Hanover Inn is open to the public and offers a unique taste of the Ivy League environment. Business meetings may be arranged at the Dartmouth College Conference Center, with support facilities at Kiewit Computation Center, where the concept of computer timesharing originated.

LAMBERTVILLE STATION

Lambertville Station, an historic 1867 railroad terminal, was originally designed by the same architect who designed the U.S. Capitol dome. Though the station has been converted into a restaurant, you can still board a sightseeing train there for a sentimental journey.

The Inn itself, in colonial brick country manor style, is filled with antiques. Each individually decorated room offers a different ambience—British Crown Colony Hong Kong, Creole New Orleans or 1920s Paris Left Bank, to mention a few. The famous New York Suite is done in "Colonial Americana" replete with empire furnishings including a rosewood highboy and a harpsichord converted into a desk.

Attentive personal service begins with a complimentary continental breakfast and newspaper, and finishes the day with nightly turndown service and Swiss chocolate on your pillow.

Lambertville Station restaurant features creative American cuisine. Dinner might begin with their celebrated hors d'oeuvre, the Alligator, followed by tropical salad, and as an entree, veal chantrelle. For dessert try strawberry sabayon or, if your appetite is hearty, apple pecan pie. The lively stationhouse bar features dancing to live entertainment. Don't miss the house specialty drink, the Station Break.

Located just 35 miles north of Philadelphia, historic Lambertville is bordered by three bodies of water—the Delaware River, the Delaware-Raritan Canal and Swan Creek. Just across the Delaware River is New Hope, Pennsylvania; both towns are famed for their fine antique shops.

The Inn at Lambertville Station
Address: 11 Bridge St., Lambertville 08530
Phone No.: 609-397-4400
Toll-free Cable: 800-524-1091
Rates: $
Credit Cards: AmEx, Visa, MC, CB, DC
No. of Rooms: 45 **Suites:** 8
Services and Amenities: Valet service, Laundry, Parking, Baby-sitting service, Complimentary newspaper, Cable TV, Radio, Whirlpool, Complimentary toiletries
Restrictions: No pets; handicapped access to 2 rooms
Concierge: 9:00 a.m.-8:00 p.m.
Room Service: 6:00 a.m.-Noon
Restaurant: Lambertville Station, Mon.-Thur. 11:30 a.m.-10:00 p.m., Fri.-Sat. 11:30 a.m.-11:00 p.m., Sun. 10:30 a.m.-10:00 p.m.
Bar: 11:30 a.m.-2:00 a.m.
Business Facilities: Copiers, Audio-visual, Teleconferencing
Conference Rooms: 2, capacity 175
Sports Facilities: Access to health spa
Location: 10 mi. off Rt. 95, Trenton/Lambertville Exit, airport transportation available
Attractions: Antique shops, factory outlets, Peddler's Village, near Princeton and Washington's Crossing

THE BISHOP'S LODGE

Address: P.O. Box 2367, Santa Fe 87504
Phone No.: 505-983-6377
Rates: $
No. of Rooms: 65 **Suites:** 19
Services and Amenities: Valet service, Laundry, Library, TV, Complimentary toiletries
Restrictions: No pets; no handicapped access
Room Service: Breakfast, lunch and dinner
Restaurant: Main Dining Room, 3 meals, Dress Code
Bar: El Charro, evenings
Business Facilities: Copiers, Audio-visual
Conference Rooms: 5, capacity 200
Sports Facilities: 4 tennis courts, skeet and trap shooting, hiking, access to golf club
Location: North boundary of Santa Fe, Tesuque district, 3 mi. north of Plaza on Washington St.
Attractions: Historic Santa Fe, art market, Indian Market, pueblos and ruins, river rafting, ghost towns

The Bishop's Lodge is secluded on nearly 1,000 acres of pinyon and juniper hills at the foot of the Sangre de Cristo Mountains, three miles north of Santa Fe in the exclusive Tesuque district. The main Lodge hacienda was built amid 17th-Century Franciscan monastery orchards as a retreat for Santa Fe's first Archbishop. The Bishop's Lodge has been owned and operated by the Thorpe family for the past seven decades.

Each comfortably appointed guest room has hand-carved furniture and a kiva fireplace, as well as a patio with lounge furniture from which to contemplate the magnificent setting. The bathrooms, colorfully decorated in Mexican tile, are thoughtfully provided with fine quality toiletries.

This is a family-oriented resort, and children are most welcome. The fine range of activities includes swimming in the bubbling spa waters and horseback riding on desert and mountain trails. There are five championship tennis courts, skeet and trap shooting, and guest privileges for golf at the Santa Fe Country Club.

The main dining room decor features Navaho rugs, Mexican chandeliers and four life-sized R. E. Rollins paintings. The cuisine is continental with a southwestern flavor. A dinner last summer consisted of guacamole de Santa Fe, Caesar salad, chilled vichyssoise, carne asada al Obispo (grilled beef tenderloin with green chili sauce and cheddar cheese), and a lovely chocolate mousse. Guests congregate by evening in the El Charro Bar, decorated with Mexican and American cowboy gear and featuring a copper-canopied fireplace. A guitarist, harpist, Mariachi, or Latin band supplies evening entertainment as guests sip marguerltas.

The Bishop's Lodge is within a few minutes' drive of several Indian pueblos, over 100 Santa Fe plaza district galleries, the vast Pecos Wilderness and the world-famous Opera.

HOTEL PLAZA ATHENEE

New York City's Hotel Plaza Athenee captures the spirit of its renowned sister hotel in Paris. This former penthouse apartment hotel, on a quiet residential street on the upper East Side, has been redesigned by architect John Carl Warnecke. The result is a unique small luxury establishment offering the type of personal service for which only a few European hotels, including the Plaza Athenee's French namesake, are justly famous.

Interiors were done by Valerian Rybar and Daigre Design Corporation. Each room is richly appointed and beautifully decorated using Swiss Zumsteg fabrics. Such features as upholstered headboards, Irish Navan carpets and Directoire night tables set the tone. Most rooms also have wet bars, stoves and refrigerators, and safe deposit boxes. Baths are clad in Portuguese marble; Porthault bathrobes, hair dryers, scales, telephones and lovely Nina Ricci toiletries are provided.

Among the exquisite suites, the most notable are two duplex suites on the top stories. Each has a living room and a dining room downstairs and bedrooms upstairs. A solarium adjoining the bedroom commands a stunning roofscape view of Manhattan.

Le Regence restaurant has 12-foot-high vaulted ceilings, handwoven carpets and imported English chandeliers. Its delightful specialties are the creations of France-trained chef Daniel Boulud.

Address: 37 East 64th St., New York 10021
Phone No.: 212-734-9100
Toll-free Cable: 800-223-5672
Telex: 6972900
Reservation Services: Leading Hotels of the World, 800-223-5672
Rates: $$$*
Credit Cards: All major credit cards
No. of Rooms: 202 **Suites:** 39
Services and Amenities: Valet service, Car hire, Laundry, Complimentary shoeshine, House doctor, Baby-sitting service, Complimentary newspaper, Cable TV, Radio, Porthault bath robes, Nina Ricci toiletries, Hair dryer, Scales, Phones
Restrictions: Small pets allowed; handicapped access to 1 room
Concierge: 24 hours
Room Service: 24 hours
Restaurant: Le Regence, 7:30 a.m.-10:30 p.m., Dress Code
Bar: Lounge
Business Facilities: Message center, Secretarial service, Translators, Copiers, Audio-visual, Telex
Sports Facilities: Health club can be arranged by concierge
Location: Between Park and Madison Avenues
Attractions: Famous boutiques, museum and gallery district, near business district

THE MAYFAIR REGENT

Address: 610 Park Avenue, New York 10021
Phone No.: 212-288-0800
Toll-free Cable: 800-223-0542
Telex: 236257 MAY UR
Reservation Services: Regent International Hotels, 800-545-4000
Rates: $$$*
Credit Cards: AmEx, DC, Visa, MC, CB
No. of Rooms: 200 **Suites:** 120
Services and Amenities: Valet service, Laundry, Car hire, International currency exchange, Complimentary shoeshine, House doctor, Robes, Soaps and Creams, Neutrogena shampoo and soap, Vitabath, Woolite, Sewing kit, Complimentary newspaper, Cable TV
Restrictions: Small pets (extra charge); handicapped access to 1 room
Concierge: 24 hours
Room Service: 24 hours
Restaurant: Le Cirque, 12:00-2:45 p.m., 6:00-10:30 p.m., Dress Code
Bar: Lobby Lounge, 11:00 a.m.-1:00 a.m.
Business Facilities: Message center, Secretarial service, Translators, Copiers, Audio-visual, Telex
Conference Rooms: 2
Sports Facilities: Health spa close by
Location: Upper East Side
Attractions: Boutique shopping, walking distance to Central Park and good restaurants

On the corner of Park Avenue and 65th Street, The Mayfair Regent is within walking distance of Madison Avenue but seems a world apart. From the minute the doorman admits you to the luxuriously understated lobby, you will find yourself in an environment of quiet dignity and effortless style. The concierge stands ready 24 hours a day to assist in making your wishes come true—from theatre tickets to seats on the Concorde.

The spacious, elegantly appointed guest rooms, in warm colors accented by fresh flowers, feature large writing desks and walk-in closets. Crabtree and Evelyn soaps and creams await you in the bathroom, as do bath robes. A favorite suite has two marble bathrooms, a wood-burning fireplace in the living room, and a magnificent view of Park Avenue.

The Lobby Lounge is a popular meeting place for breakfast, lunch or traditional European afternoon tea, served from 3:00 to 6:00 p.m. daily. Guests may enjoy delicious scones, pound cake with citron and an assortment of finger sandwiches.

One of New York's most fashionable and celebrated restaurants, Le Cirque, is located here. 24-hour room service is also available. Educated in Italy and India, General Manager Dario Mariotti has developed his professional skills in a number of Europe's finest hotels. He strives to maintain exceptional standards of service and style, and Mr. Mariotti's standards are quite high indeed.

THE LOWELL

Address: 28 East 63rd St., New York 10021
Phone No.: 212-838-1400
Telex: 275750 LOWL/UR
Rates: $$$*
Credit Cards: All major credit cards
No. of Rooms: 60 **Suites:** 52
Services and Amenities: Valet service, Complimentary shoeshine, Guests given temporary membership to backgammon club, Complimentary newspaper, Cable TV, Phone in bath, Robes, Soaps, Shampoo, Conditioners, Hand lotion
Restrictions: No handicapped access
Concierge: 24 hours
Room Service: 7:00 a.m.-2:00 a.m.
Restaurant: The Pembroke Room, 7:00 a.m.-11:00 a.m., Noon-3:00 p.m., 4:00-7:00 p.m.
Bar: The Post House, same hours as restaurant
Conference Rooms: Small meeting for 8-10 can be arranged in suite
Location: Upper East Side, 30 min. from La Guardia, 1 hr. from JFK Airport
Attractions: Madison Ave. shopping, Museums, Central Park

One of New York's most recently and elaborately restored small grand luxe hotels, The Lowell is centrally located in an upper East Side neighborhood of townhouses and quiet tree-lined streets. Nearby are the city's finest boutiques, restaurants and galleries as well as several Fortune 500 corporations' headquarters.

The facade is art deco, and the atmosphere mingles Roaring Twenties nostalgia with thoroughly modern opulence. Empire furniture with gold ormolu mounts sets the tone in the intentionally low-key lobby.

Nearly all of the 60 guest rooms are suites. Luxuriously furnished in eclectic style, each reminds one of the sort of elegant *pied-a-terre* one would hope to find in Rome or Paris. Many have fireplaces and all have kitchens. The walls, floors and vanities are of travertine, accented with gleaming brass fixtures and fresh flowers.

The tiny 35-seat Pembroke Room, on the hotel's second floor, provides an intimate place for breakfast or lunch and a very special spot in which to enjoy high tea. Gourmet dining is to be found in The Post House, a favorite New York "watering hole".

Perhaps the most extraordinary feature of this warm and delightful little hotel is its thoughtful, highly professional staff—who outnumber the guests by two to one!

THE PIERRE

The legendary French chef Charles Pierre Casalasco had dreamed of opening a European-style luxury hotel on New York's Fifth Avenue, and his dream came true in 1930 with the unveiling of The Pierre, then hailed as "a monument of beauty and one of the most majestic structures in all New York." Overlooking Central Park, the imposing Georgian structure capped by a gleaming copper tower was inspired by a French chateau.

Half a century after Pierre's death, his dream hotel has been restored and redecorated by Valerian Rybar and Rosalie Wise with scrupulous attention to detail and personal service that would have made the Frenchman glow with pride.

Each of the rooms is individually and exquisitely furnished. Such services as manned elevators, twice-daily maid service, valet and hand laundry, rare in today's world, are regular features here. Special preferences of guests are noted by the staff and remembered on return visits. The multi-lingual concierge can accomplish feats that range from chartering a private plane to procuring gourmet delicacies not listed on the day's menu.

The Cafe Pierre and the Pierre Bar are New York classics. A recent pre-theatre menu began with smoked Scotch salmon, followed by oxtail consomme and a sampler of seasonal salads. The entrees were roast of the day served from a silver trolley, and Turbot with pistachios and pine nuts. The choice of desserts was chocolate terrine or lemon mousse with raspberry coulis. The wine list, of course, is sensational.

This is a fine example of a classic hotel thoughtfully and delightfully updated to become a landmark 20th-Century hostelry.

Address: 2 East 61st Street, New York 10021

Phone No.: 212-838-8000
Toll-free Cable: 800-268-8282

Reservation Service: Leading Hotels of the World

Rates: $$$$*

Credit Cards: AmEx, CB, MC, DC, Visa, Air Canada, JCB

No. of Rooms: 196 **Suites:** 45

Services and Amenities: Valet service, Barber shop, Beauty shop, Garage and parking, Car hire, International currency exchange, Complimentary shoeshine, House doctor, Baby-sitting service, Laundry, Complimentary newspaper, Cable TV, Radio, Shampoo, Gelee, Shower cap, Shoehorn, Shoeshine mitt

Restrictions: Small pets on leash; no handicapped access

Concierge: 7:00 a.m.-11:00 p.m.

Room Service: 24 hours

Restaurant: Cafe Pierre, 7:00 a.m.-11:30 p.m., Dress Code; The Rotunda

Bar: Pierre Bar, 11:30 a.m.-1:00 a.m.

Business Facilities: Secretarial service

Conference Rooms: 7, capacity 1500

Location: Midtown-8 mi. from La Guardia, 15 Miles from JFK, 6 blocks west of FDR Drive

Attractions: Within walking distance of Fifth Avenue shops, boutiques, museums and galleries

MORGANS

Address: 237 Madison Avenue, New York 10016
Phone No.: 212-686-0300
Toll-free Cable: 800-334-3408
Telex: 288908
Rates: $$$*
Credit Cards: AmEx, Visa, MC, DC
No. of Rooms: 154 **Suites:** 28
Services and Amenities: Valet service, Library, Garage and parking, Car hire, Currency exchange, Complimentary shoeshine, Babysitting service, Laundry, Complimentary newspaper, Complimentary breakfast, Cable TV, VCR, Stereo cassette, Radio, Telephone, Complimentary toiletries
Restrictions: Pets limited; handicapped access to 2 rooms
Concierge: 24 hours
Room Service: 24 hours
Restaurant: Morgans Restaurant, 11:30 a.m.-1:00 a.m.
Bar: Morgans, 11:30 a.m.-1:00 a.m.
Business Facilities: Message center, Secretarial service, Copiers, Telex
Conference Rooms: 1 small meeting room
Location: Murray Hill area
Attractions: Near theatres, shopping and museums, fashion district, Empire State Building

Developed by Steve Rubell of Studio 54 fame, Morgans is a hotel that tries not to seem like one. The informal atmosphere strives for a "home-away-from-home" feel incorporating today's finest design sensibilities, from highly stylized decor innovations by Andree Putman to staff uniforms by Calvin Klein and Giorgio Armani. The exceptionally high staff-to-guest ratio insures that all guests' whims are satisfied.

Of the 154 rooms, 28 are suites. Furniture is covered in Brooks Brothers pin-striped shirt material and grey flannel men's suit fabrics. Walls are finished with speckled spray-on Zolatone ("Monet in a can") in subtle hues. Each room features an original avante-garde Robert Mapplethorpe photograph. Custom-built wall units house stereo cassette systems and VCRs, and the hotel has an on-premises video tape library. The baths fulfill Ms. Putman's goal to "design an incredible bathroom without being obliged to use marble" through Japanese black and white wall tiles, stainless steel sinks and seamless poured granite floors.

Morgans Restaurant is owned and operated by Larry Forgione, who is also chef/owner of Manhattan's legendary An American Place. His totally unique menu, in keeping with the hotel's style of offbeat excellence, focuses on "fun finger food" including grilled shrimp in peanut sauce, oysters on the half shell, buffalo chicken wings, and smoked salmon tartare on toast.

As a final fillip, guests are guaranteed admission to The Palladium, New York's most sought-after jet set night spot.

RITZ-CARLTON

This classic hotel, first opened in 1930, has been brilliantly refurbished under the direction of designer Sister Parish (Mrs. Henry Parish II) of the Parish-Hadley design firm. Mr. John B. Coleman's desire to produce a New York City hotel that would both merit and enhance the Ritz-Carlton name has been realized in this, the quintessence of elegance.

The atmosphere is reminiscent of that to be found in an elite London club. The authentic wood panelling, accented by 18th century animal and equestrian prints, sets the design motif carried throughout the hotel with Chippendale style furnishings and myriad pictures on all available wall space.

All guest rooms are exquisitely appointed to create a fine residential flavor suggesting a somewhat idealized version of golden age English country life. Each uniquely decorated room features antique reproductions and an eclectic array of colors, patterns and textures to intrigue the eye.

The intimate Jockey Club Restaurant glows with soft red upholstery and carpeting, polished knotty pine and 18th- and 19th-Century English sport paintings. Tables are set with gold-rimmed Spode china and fresh flowers.

The service here is impeccable, the location beautiful and the experience not to be missed.

Address: 112 Central Park South, New York 10019
Phone No.: 212-757-1900
Toll-free Cable: 800-223-7990
Telex: 971534
Reservation Services: 212-838-3110 collect
Rates: $$$*
Credit Cards: All major credit cards
No. of Rooms: 237 **Suites:** 35
Services and Amenities: Valet service, Garage and parking, Laundry, Car hire, Currency exchange, Complimentary shoeshine, Baby-sitting service, Complimentary newspaper, Cable TV, Radio, 3 phones with 2 lines, Robes, Sun lamps
Restrictions: No pets; handicapped access to 14 rooms
Concierge: 8:00 a.m.-10:00 p.m.
Room Service: 24 hours
Restaurant: Jockey Club, 7:00 a.m.-Midnight, Dress Code
Bar: Jockey Club, opens 11:00 a.m.
Business Facilities: Message center, Secretarial service, Translators, Copiers, Audio-visual, Telex
Conference Rooms: 4, capacity 150
Location: Midtown Manhattan, 15 mi. from JFK Airport, 5 mi. from highway
Attractions: Adjacent to Central Park

GREEN PARK INN

Address: Highway 321 South, P.O. Box 7, Blowing Rock 28605
Phone No.: 704-295-3141
Rates: $
Credit Cards: MC, Visa, AmEx
No. of Rooms: 78 **Suites:** 10
Services and Amenities: Babysitting service, Laundry, Complimentary newspaper, TV, Telephone
Restrictions: Pets with prior approval
Concierge: Afternoons-Evenings
Room Service: Hours vary
Restaurant: Main Dining Room, Garden Room, 7:00-9:00 a.m., Noon-2:00 p.m., 6:00-9:00 p.m.
Bar: Divide Lounge, Noon-Midnight
Business Facilities: Message center, Secretarial service, Copier, Audio-visual
Conference Rooms: 5, capacity 200
Sports Facilities: 3 tennis courts, 18-hole golf course, hiking, skiing, whitewater rafting, canoeing available close by
Location: Mountain resort village
Attractions: Appalachian State University Summer Cultural Festival, Grandfather Mountain, Glendale Springs

Green Park Inn, one of the South's oldest luxury resorts, has been in continuous operation since 1882 and is listed on the National Register of Historic Places. The stately white frame Victorian manor is a world unto itself. Situated 4,300 feet up in the Blue Ridge Mountains, Green Park Inn is known for cool summer breezes and delightful atmosphere.

High tea is served on the veranda. The Inn's reputation for fine food is exemplified by such specialties as blackened red fish, roast Carolina duckling, and mushrooms stuffed with crab. Later you may enjoy dancing to the Green Park Big Band and sip the house special drink, Mimosa.

Board meetings and business conferences are a specialty. After work is over, you and your colleagues will enjoy guest privileges at the neighboring Blowing Rock Country Club.

The Inn is, first and foremost, a vacation paradise for lovers of the outdoors. Horseback riding, hiking, hanggliding, fishing and a scenic steam locomotive trip are all nearby. Grandfather Mountain and Linville Gorge, among the South's last untouched wilderness areas, offer the adventurous a rare opportunity to see black bears, cougars, deer and bald eagles in their natural habitat. And believe it or not, wintertime guests also find excellent ski slopes just down the road.

REGISTRY INN

Charlotte's Registry Inn is dedicated to excellence and first-class service in the gracious European tradition. Centrally located in the airport area, The Registry is near all of Charlotte's business destinations.

Each guest room has either English or French style traditional furnishings, overstuffed Queen Anne chairs, Italian marble tables, a spacious writing desk and an armoire fitted with cable TV and AM-FM stereo.

The elegant La Tache Restaurant, decorated in subdued peach, green and rose hues, has a country French ambience. Tables are set with Villeroy & Bach china in the Palermo pattern. Dinner may begin with a salad of radicchio, hearts of palm and Belgian endive in watercress with lime-hazelnut dressing; next, lobster bisque with morel mushrooms and caviar; as an entree, rack of spring lamb with Dijon mustard and herbs; and to top it off, strawberries Romanoff. The adjoining La Tache Lounge offers a lighter menu and, later in the evening, dancing to live entertainment.

The beautifully landscaped grounds feature a pool with a unique handcrafted sundeck. Guests are also extended privileges to the Charlotte Health and Racquetball Club, and many take advantage of the nearby jogging trails.

The smallest and most intimate of the Registry Hotels, the Inn makes a special effort to provide genuinely elegant touches and personal service.

Address: 321 West Woodlawn Road, Charlotte 28210
Phone No.: 704-525-4441
Toll-free Cable: NC 800-532-0593, US 800-438-1376
Telex: 802195
Reservation Services: Sabre, Pars & Apollo
Rates: $
Credit Cards: Visa, MC, AmEx, DC, CB
No. of Rooms: 181 **Suites:** 4
Services and Amenities: Valet service, Free parking, Baby-sitting service, Gift shop, Complimentary newspaper, Cable TV, Robes, Radio, Bath oil, Shampoo, Shoe mitt
Restrictions: No pets; handicapped access to 5 rooms
Concierge: 24 hours
Room Service: 24 hours
Restaurant: La Tache, 6:30 a.m.-2:00 p.m., 6:00-11:00 p.m., Dress Code
Bar: La Tache Lounge, Mon.-Sat. 11:00 a.m.-1:00 a.m., Sun. Noon-11:00 p.m.
Business Facilities: Message center, Copiers, Audio-visual, Teleconferencing, Telex
Conference Rooms: 5, capacity 15-200
Sports Facilities: Heated swimming pool, whirlpool
Attractions: Cannon Mills Village, Discover Place, Heritage USA, Mint Museum, Spirit Square

VERNON MANOR

Address: 400 Oak Street, Cincinnati 45219
Phone No.: 513-281-3300
Toll-free Cable: 800-543-3999
Rates: $*
Credit Cards: AmEx, Visa, MC, DC, CB
No. of Rooms: 120 **Suites:** 10
Services and Amenities: Gift shop, Valet service, Barber shop, Laundry, Garage and parking, Complimentary newspaper, TV, Radio, Vitabath, Shampoo
Restrictions: No pets; no handicapped access
Room Service: Yes
Restaurant: The Forum, 11:00 a.m.-2:30 p.m., 5:00-10:00 p.m.; Cardigans Cafe, 7:00-11:00 a.m., 11:00 a.m.-5:00 p.m., 5:00-10:00 p.m.
Bar: Beagles Lounge, 11:00 a.m.-1:00 a.m.
Business Facilities: Copiers, Audio-visual, Teleconferencing
Conference Rooms: 7, capacity 150
Location: University District, 15 mi. north of airport, 2 blocks west of I-71
Attractions: Zoo, art museum, natural history museum, Cincinnati Reds and Bengals

This hotel has been the home-away-from-home choice in Cincinnati for guests including The Beatles, Nancy Reagan, George Bush, John F. Kennedy and Anthony Quinn. Built in 1924 in a unique Elizabethan style patterned after Hatfield House in Hertfordshire, England, The Vernon Manor is dedicated to its guests' relaxation and total satisfaction.

The Vernon Manor is uptown, on a tree-lined street in one of Cincinnati's Historic Districts, within five minutes from the business and entertainment destinations of downtown Cincinnati.

The spacious guest rooms are beautifully furnished in mahogany and brass, with a deep blue and beige color scheme accented by hunt pictures. A favorite suite, the Baryshnikov, is sufficiently opulent to satisfy even the most discriminating visitor.

The Forum dining room radiates Old World charm and elegance. The menu, mixing the best in continental cuisine with American classics, offers such delights as mushroom caps stuffed with crabmeat, Caesar salad, tournedos Oscar, and chocolate truffle cake. There is a fine wine list from which to choose.

After dinner, visit the Beagles Lounge—an English pub if ever there was one, with whimsical paintings of dogs, hunter green carpeting and comfortable club chairs. The bar hosts nationally acclaimed jazz groups and has a dance floor. It also has the longest (and most convivial) happy hour in Cincinnati.

Guests are extended privileges to the Friars Club.

Business meetings are a specialty at The Vernon Manor, and the hotel's conference facilities can accommodate parties and banquets for up to 250 people. The staff is prepared to help make your event memorable, and equipment is available for every presentation need.

WATERFORD HOTEL

Officially opened in 1985, the new Waterford Hotel is situated within a 37-acre development in exclusive northwest Oklahama City. The hotel's architecture, designed by the Architectural Compendium of Oklahoma City with attentive personal supervision by developer Charles S. Givens, is in fine traditional style. Locally produced deep red brick, iron and wood give the Waterford its "made-in-Oklahoma" feel.

Classical elements abound throughout, featuring Italian peach marble and dark green marble. Red travertine is used extensively in the baths. All design elements are unified and are carried through into the guest rooms, which have mahogany high post or ribbon bed frames and subtly lush colors. Beds are luxuriously made up with three all-cotton sheets and feather pillows. Ample amenities include overnight shoeshine, fine bath toiletries and electronic keyless locks and evening turndown.

The Waterford Restaurant is an elegant formal mahogany-panelled room. Tables are dressed with Bauscher china and Sambonet silverware. A recent dinner began with deep fried artichoke hearts stuffed with crayfish tails on oyster hollandaise. The second course was Bookbinder red snapper soup, followed by spinach salad with hot bacon and chanterrelles dressing. The entrees were Florida pompano and lobster medallions in Cabernet Sauvignon sauce en papillote, and roast rack of lamb with mustard seed. For dessert, Viennese apple strudel with warm vanilla sauce.

Afternoon tea, a growing Oklahoma City tradition, is served in both the Waterford Lounge and the hotel lobby. Included are over a dozen varieties of tea and an array of sweets, scones and tiny sandwiches.

Sports possibilities are many, with a swimming pool in a garden setting, two tennis courts, two squash courts and full health spa facilities. Golf, riding and sailing are available nearby.

The Waterford Hotel has brought a new world of resort-style hospitality to Oklahoma City.

Address: 6300 Waterford Boulevard, Oklahoma City 73118
Phone No.: 405-848-4782
Toll-free cable: 800-522-9440 OK, 800-992-2009 US
Telex: 796026 Vista OKC
Rates: $*
Credit Cards: All major credit cards plus JCB
No. of Rooms: 196 **Suites:** 32
Services and Amenities: Valet service, Garage and parking, Complimentary shoeshine, Laundry, Baby-sitting service, Complimentary newspaper, Cable TV Spectradyne, Phone in bath, Shampoo, Bath gel, Shoe mitt, Sewing kit
Restrictions: No pets; handicapped access to 2 rooms
Room Service: 24 hours
Restaurant: Waterford Restaurant, lunch and dinner; Veranda Restaurant, breakfast, lunch and dinner. Dress Code
Bar: Waterford Lounge, 11:30 a.m.-1:30 a.m., Closed Sunday
Business Facilities: Audio-visual
Conference Rooms: Grand Ballroom, capacity 750; Chapter Room, capacity 250; Each of 7 guest room floors has conference space
Sports Facilities: 2 hard-surface tennis courts, 2 squash courts, golf, riding and sailing nearby, full health spa, Nautilus
Location: Northwest Oklahoma City, 14 mi. from airport, 2 min. from I-44
Attractions: Museum of Art, Art Center, National Cowboy Hall of Fame, Western Heritage Center, Oklahoma Zoo, Omniplex Shopping Center

SKIRVIN PLAZA

Address: One Park Avenue, Oklahoma City 73102
Phone No.: 405-232-4411
Reservation Services: 800-323-7500
Rates: $*
Credit Cards: AmEx, CB, DC, MC, Visa
No. of Rooms: 208 **Suites:** 10
Services and Amenities: Valet service, Beauty shop, Garage and parking, Complimentary shoeshine, House doctor, Complimentary newspaper, Cable TV, Telephone
Restrictions: Small pets only; handicapped access to 2 rooms
Room Service: 7:30 a.m.-10:30 p.m.
Restaurant: Park Avenue Room, 6:30 a.m.-11:00 p.m., Dress Code; Great American Cafe, Mon.-Fri. 7:00 a.m.-2:00 p.m.
Bar: Palm Court, 11:00 a.m.-Midnight
Business Facilities: Secretarial service, Copiers, Audio-visual, Teleconferencing, Telex
Conference Rooms: 11, capacity 3,500
Sports Facilities: Guest privileges at YMCA
Location: Downtown Oklahoma City

The Skirvin Plaza, built in 1911 in elegantly traditional style, was the dream of Big Bill Skirvin, oil man, land baron and cattle king. Mr. Skirvin was also the architect. Today The Skirvin Plaza reflects Oklahoma City's renaissance in the gorgeous lobby hung with crystal chandeliers and supported by massive, elaborately carved oak pillars.

The rooms are spacious and quite well appointed. The Skirvin Plaza also has unique Tower Floors especially designed for the business traveler, with such extras as a concierge, executive cocktail lounge and access to many business services.

The Park Avenue Room restaurant is an Oklahoma City institution. The elegant tone is set by tables graced with long-stemmed roses in silver glasses. The continental cuisine is excellent. The Great American Cafe, open for breakfast and lunch Monday through Friday, offers a more casual atmosphere.

The Palm Court Lounge piano bar adjacent to the lobby is where guests tend to congregate for complimentary hors d'oeuvres and music.

Recent visitors to the hotel have included President Ronald Reagan, operatic tenor Luciano Pavarotti, and Shirley Jones (who, you may recall, achieved her stardom in "Oklahoma"). Whether you travel for business or pleasure, you will find The Skirvin Plaza Hotel a true Oklahoma original.

SALISHAN LODGE

Located on the scenic Central Oregon coast, Salishan Lodge has evolved as the *ne plus ultra* of meeting places for groups of from 20 to 500. The Lodge's light and airy conference facilities feature the latest in audio-visual communication equipment, including built-in screens and blackout curtains.

150 spacious and well-appointed guest rooms, with hush-quiet soundproofing and covered parking, surround the main lodge. Each room has its own fireplace, ready to use upon arrival, and a balcony offering a lovely view of Gleneden Beach, the Lodge's landscaped grounds or the evergreen forests.

The cuisine at Salishan is consistently rated among the finest in the Northwest. As an example, a recent dinner in the dining room consisted of chinook salmon poached and served with a sauce Chardonnay, julienne of spinach salad, and medallions of veal Salishan. Groups can enjoy a salmon barbecue on one of the large patios.

Golf at Salishan follows the original Scottish tradition of ocean-side greens. The 18-hole course will please both novices and pros. The large indoor pool is kept at a delightful 80 degrees year-round. Besides outdoor tennis courts, there is a three-court indoor tennis club. The fitness and recreation center has the latest in exercise equipment, as well as Jacuzzis and sauna.

700 acres of woodland preserve, adjoining boundless wild forest, offer miles of trails for running and hiking. Over 2½ miles of private shoreline are ideal for beachcombing.

Address: Gleneden Beach 97388
Phone No.: 503-764-3600
Toll-free Cable: US 800-547-6500
Rates: $*
Credit Cards: Visa, AmEx, MC, DC, CB
No. of Rooms: 151 **Suites:** 3
Services and Amenities: Covered parking, Car hire, House doctor, Baby-sitting service, Game area, Laundry, Complimentary newspaper, TV, Radio, Soap, Shower gel, Shampoo
Restrictions: Extra charge for pet; handicapped access to 2 rooms
Concierge: 8:00 a.m.-6:00 p.m.
Room Service: Yes
Restaurant: The Salishan Dining Room, 6:00 a.m.-11:00 p.m., Dress Code
Bar: Attic Lounge, 2:00 p.m.-2:00 a.m.
Business Facilities: Message center-front desk, Copiers, Audio-visual, Meeting planner's office arranges secretarial service
Conference Rooms: 10, capacity 10-500
Sports Facilities: 3 indoor, 1 outdoor tennis court, 18-hole golf course, whirlpool, sauna, weight training
Location: Central Oregon coast
Attractions: Scenic coast, deep-sea salmon fishing

COLUMBIA GORGE HOTEL

Address: 4000 West Cliff Drive, Hood River 97031
Phone No.: 503-386-5566
Toll-free Cable: OR 800-826-4027, Western US 800-345-1921
Credit Cards: DC, AmEx, MC, Visa
No. of Rooms: 46 **Suites:** 4
Services and Amenities: Gift shop, Parking, Laundry, Complimentary shoeshine, Baby-sitting service, Complimentary newspaper, Cable TV, Phone
Restrictions: Handicapped access to 2 rooms
Room Service: 8:00 a.m.-9:00 p.m.
Restaurant: Columbia Court, 8:00-11:00 a.m., 11:00 a.m.-3:00 p.m., 5:00-11:00 p.m.
Bar: Valentino Lounge, 8:00 a.m.-2:00 a.m.
Business Facilities: Copiers, Audio-visual
Conference Rooms: 2, capacity 40-150
Sports Facilities: 9-hole golf course 1 mi., tennis courts ½ mi., whitewater rafting, summer skiing, salmon fishing, hiking
Location: From Portland I-84 to Exit 62, from Airport I-205 to I-84 East to Exit 62
Attractions: Blossom Festival each April, View of Mt. Hood

The Columbia Gorge Hotel was built in 1921 on a cliff above the mighty Columbia River at the foot of majestic Mount Hood and quickly became a favorite retreat for the jazz-age rich and famous. Now listed on the National Register of Historic Places, the hotel continues to delight visitors with its spectacular natural setting and superlative service.

The spacious guest rooms, individually decorated with original art, offer a choice of brass or canopy beds. Evening turndown service comes with a rose as well as a chocolate.

The world-famous Farm Breakfast, a multi-course extravaganza, is definitely worth waking up for. The Columbia River Court dining room serves fine Northwestern cuisine, like fresh Columbia River salmon, dry-aged Eastern prime beef and Hood River apple pie, in classic 20's Country Inn style.

The multitude of outdoor activity possibilities includes river rafting, water sports, skiing on Mt. Hood, fishing, hiking and more. The waterfall that plunges from the hotel's "backyard" to the river 206 feet below has been the scene of romantic interludes for generations of visitors.

The Columbia Gorge Hotel is a favorite conference locale for small high level meetings. Every effort is made throughout the hotel to provide thoughtful service; the staff is dedicated to making each guest's visit—whether for business or pleasure—a memorable one.

While in the area, be sure to visit the Maryhill Museum with its world-renowned collection of Rodin sculptures.

HEATHMAN HOTEL

This National Historic Landmark in downtown Portland is next door to the Center for the Performing Arts and just a few steps from the Art Museum and downtown business and shopping districts.

The Heathman was completely renovated in 1984 under the supervision of San Francisco's master interior designer, Andrew Delfino. Original works by leading American artists are displayed throughout the hotel. The lobby, featuring rare eucalyptus panelling, a grand piano and a fireplace, is the setting for afternoon tea, a burgeoning Portland custom.

Each spacious guest room is decorated with teak wood and art deco furnishings. Carrara white and Verona red marble, Roman travertine and Burmese teak have been artfully blended to create an unabashedly luxurious decor. Rooms have VCRs to enjoy movies from the hotel's large film library. Baths are fitted with marble and provided with robes and abundant complimentary toiletries.

The Heathman has become a Portland dining favorite, thanks in part to its proximity to cultural events. The restaurant prides itself on serving the finest and freshest Northwest regional seafood, vegetables and meat. Menus change seasonally; in the spring, dinner began with Northwest game pate wth red remoulade sauce, then the Heathman salad of Romaine, butter lettuce, garlic croutons, bacon and mint tossed together in a delectable dressing. The entree was rack of Oregon lamb, and dessert a chocolate raspberry torte served along with the Heathman's house blend coffee.

The elegant Marble Bar, named for its exquisite marble furnishings, is a popular apres-theatre meeting place, serving tapas-style hors d'oeuvres until 2:00 a.m.

The care and thought that have gone into refurbishing this hotel, combined with courteous professional service, will surely please.

Address: 1009 Southwest Broadway, Portland 97205
Phone No.: 503-241-4100
Toll-free Cable: 800-323-7500
Rates: $$
Credit Cards: Visa, MC, AmEx, CB, DC
No. of Rooms: 120 **Suites:** 40
Services and Amenities: Gift shop, Valet service, Laundry, Garage and parking, Car hire, Currency exchange, Baby-sitting service, Video library, Complimentary newspaper, TV, VCR, Radio, Phone, Robes, Complimentary toiletries
Restrictions: No pets except Seeing Eye dogs; handicapped access to 8 rooms
Concierge: 24 hours
Room Service: 24 hours
Restaurant: Heathman Restaurant, 6:00 a.m.-10:00 p.m.
Bar: Marble Bar & Lobby Lounge, 11:00 a.m.-2:00 a.m.
Business Facilities: Complete business center, all facilities
Conference Rooms: 7, capacity 72 (seated)-150 (standing)
Sports Facilities: In-room exercise equipment available, access to athletic club
Location: Downtown, 15 mi. from airport, 1 mi. from highway
Attractions: Shopping, Performing Arts Center

THE ALEXIS

Address: 1510 Southwest Harbor Way, Portland 97201
Phone No.: 503-228-3233
Toll-free Cable: 800-227-1333
Rates: $$*
Credit Cards: AmEx, Visa, MC, CB
No. of Rooms: 74 **Suites:** 24
Services and Amenities: Valet service, Laundry, Garage and parking, Car hire, Complimentary shoeshine, Baby-sitting service, Complimentary newspaper, Cable TV, Radio, Robes, Whirlpool bath, Shampoo, Lotion, Bath gel, Sachet
Restrictions: small pets by prearrangement; handicapped access to 4 rooms
Concierge: 24 hours
Room Service: 24 hours
Restaurant: Esplanade Restaurant, 6:30 a.m.-10:00 p.m.
Bar: The Bar, 11:30 a.m.-1:00 a.m.
Business Facilities: Message center, Secretarial service, Translators, Copiers, Audio-visual, other business services available on request
Conference Rooms: 1, capacity 16
Sports Facilities: Water skiing, sailing, whirlpool, sauna
Attractions: Major city park, Esplanade walkway of shops and boutiques

European in style and service, Portland's stately new Alexis Hotel maintains a uniquely Northwestern character in its wood and brick exterior. The location, on the Willamette River at Governor Tom McCall Park in the prestigious RiverPlace neighborhood, is convenient to the downtown financial district, shopping and theatres.

The spacious rooms are well appointed with traditional furnishings that reflect the aura of warmth and comfort felt throughout the hotel. Each bath is lushly accoutered with plush towels and a basket of personal care amenities. Guests enjoy complimentary sherry upon arrival, morning newspapers, overnight shoeshine, twice-daily maid service with evening turndown, and complimentary continental breakfast.

The Esplanade Restaurant has dark blue Axminster carpeting, light wood furnishings with rose upholstery, rose china and crystal, fresh flowers and a spectacular view of the riverfront. Fine cuisine has made it a Portland favorite—be sure to try the ragout of scallops and prawns. Also in the RiverPlace Complex are the Newport Bay Restaurant (a floating eatery), McCormick & Schmik's Harborside Restaurant and the Shanghai Club Lounge, a lively spot for wining, dining and dancing.

Guests enjoy the hotel spa and whirlpool. Additional exercise facilities are available in the RiverPlace YMCA, to which guests are extended privileges.

PALACE HOTEL

In the heart of this historic American city, the parklike vistas from this elegant hotel on Logan Square may remind you of Europe. The management, under the direction of the internationally famed Trusthouse Forte Group, makes guests feel at home from a warm personal welcome to 24-hour concierge service.

All guest accommodations are suites, quite elegant suites at that. Their expanse alone, 800 square feet, sets them apart. Such touches as marble-clad bathrooms and fine furnishings help establish the home-away-from-home atmosphere.

The Cafe Royal restaurant and bar provides a formal setting in which to relax and be entertained, with live music every evening. Restaurant tables are dressed with Royal Doulton china, fresh flowers and candlelight to create a romantic dining ambience. The cuisine leaves nothing to be desired, from crayfish in puff pastry to the delicious dessert souffles—chocolate, vanilla and Grand Marnier.

There are a terrace level pool and sun deck for relaxation, as well as a sauna, and guests are extended privileges to The London Work Out health club.

The best of Philadelphia, including business, government, historic and cultural areas, is within a four-block radius of the hotel.

Address: 18th & Benjamin Franklin Parkway, Philadelphia 19103
Phone No.: 215-963-2222
Toll-free Cable: 800-223-5672
Reservation Services: THF/FOR-TRES 800-223-5672
Rates: $$
Credit Cards: AmEx, Visa, MC, DC, CB, Trusthouse Forte
No. of Suites: 285
Services and Amenities: Valet service, Laundry, Garage and parking, Car hire, Currency exchange, Complimentary shoeshine, House doctor, Baby-sitting service, Complimentary newspaper, Cable TV, Radio, Telephone, Robes, Heat lamp, Shampoo, Conditioners, Talcum powder, Hand lotion, Mouthwash
Restrictions: Kennels available through concierge; handicapped access to 5 rooms
Concierge: 24 hours
Room Service: 24 hours
Restaurant: Cafe Royal, Noon-2:00 p.m., 6:00-10:00 p.m., Dress Code
Bar: Cafe Royal Bar, until 1:00 a.m.
Business Facilities: Message center, Secretarial service, Translators, Copiers, Audio-visual, Teleconferencing, Telex
Conference Rooms: 10, capacity 150
Sports Facilities: Outdoor swimming pool, access to health club
Location: Downtown
Attractions: Walking distance to all major cultural areas

THE LATHAM

Address: 17th & Walnut St., Philadelphia 19103
Phone No.: 215-563-7474
Toll-free Cable: 800-LATHAM-1
Rates: $$
Credit Cards: Visa, MC, AmEx, DC, CB
No. of Rooms: 141
Services and Amenities: Valet service, Laundry, Garage and parking, Baby-sitting service, Complimentary newspaper, Cable TV, Video cassette players, Radio, Phone, Mini bar, Refrigerator, Complimentary toiletries, Hair dryer
Restrictions: Pets limited; no handicapped access
Concierge: Noon-8:00 p.m.
Room Service: 24 hours
Restaurant: Bogart's, 7:00 a.m.-11:00 p.m.
Bar: 11:00 a.m.-2:00 a.m.
Business Facilities: Message center, Secretarial service, Copiers, Audio-visual, Telex
Conference Rooms: 4, 1300 square feet
Sports Facilities: Access to health club
Location: Center city, 7 mi. from airport, 1 mi. from Schuylkill and I-5 highways
Attractions: Shopping, museums, antiques, theatres

Corporate travelers' accommodations in elegantly traditional style are to be found at this intimate city center hotel on prestigious Rittenhouse Square. Small size, attentive service and European ambience combine to create a warm and hospitable environment.

The newly refurbished lobby features a large crystal chandelier, marble walls and floor, and fine woodwork. Old-World European decor also graces the guest rooms, in subtle colors and finished to create a residential character. Amenities include fully stocked mini wet bars, in-room safes, hair dryers, and large baths with ample toiletries, a telephone and bathrobes. Special rooms are designed to meet the needs of women travelers. At the end of a busy day, one appreciates the nightly turndown service with a goodnight chocolate.

For relaxation, guests enjoy the full service health club.

The Latham features one of Philadelphia's finest restaurants, Bogart's, set in a Casablanca atmosphere with ceiling fans, bamboo, and banquettes. The relaxing ambience will put you in the mood to enjoy a meal such as mushrooms stuffed with crab meat, Caesar salad, champagne sorbet, crown rack of lamb with duchess potatoes, and banana flambe. After your meal, repair to the Crickett lounge for late-night entertainment.

PLANTERS INN

Charleston's historic district, the 18th-Century city market area, abounds with antique shops, restaurants, flower vendors and boutiques. The district's bed-and-breakfast inns have traditionally played an important role in visitors' enjoyment of this venerable Old South seaport; now the Planters Inn has set a whole new standard in cozy, elegant charm with courteous professional service. Designed in the manner of Charleston's fine antebellum homes, the lobby features detailed crown molding and fireplace mantle, antique furnishings and fine art. The 46 guest rooms and suites feature high ceilings, mahogany four-poster beds and tall windows draped in swags and festoons. The large bathrooms, beautifully done in travertine marble, are also equipped with telephone, TV, French milled soap and toiletries. Nightly turndown service will make you feel pampered.

Planters Inn is home to Silks restaurant, named for the collection of racing silks and equestrian paintings displayed throughout the bar and dining room. The chefs are trained in the classic French tradition, which combines with an emphasis on farm-fresh produce of the region to produce an outstanding cuisine. Some favorite dishes are she-crab soup, Silks five-leaf salad, blackened fish, and their famous Silks signature cake. The restaurant stocks nearly 300 labels of American wine in its thoroughbred wine cellar.

Address: 112 North Market Street, Charleston 29401
Phone No.: 803-722-2345
Toll-free Cable: 800-845-7082
Rates: $
Credit Cards: AmEx, Visa, MC, DC
No. of Rooms: 46 **Suites:** 5
Services and Amenities: Valet service, Barber shop, Beauty shop, Valet parking, Laundry, Complimentary shoeshine, Baby-sitting service, Complimentary newspaper, Remote control TV, Radio, Phone, Shampoo and gel, French milled soap
Restrictions: No pets; handicapped access to 2 rooms
Room Service: 7:00-11:00 p.m.
Restaurant: Silks, 7:00 a.m.-11:00 p.m.
Bar: Silks, 11:00 a.m.-1:00 a.m.
Business Facilities: Message center, Secretarial service, Copiers, Audio-visual
Conference Rooms: 1, capacity 40
Location: Historic district-from airport south on I-27 to Meeting Street, south to corner of Meeting and Market
Attractions: Historic market and antique district outside front door; Spoleto Music Festival, May 24 to June 29 annually; spring and fall tours of homes

THE HERMITAGE

Address: 231 Sixth Avenue North, Nashville 37219
Phone No.: 615-244-3121
Toll-free Cable: US 800-251-1908, TN 800-342-1816
Reservation Service: Park Suite Hotels, 800-822-2323
Rates: $
Credit Cards: AmEx, MC, Visa, CB, DC
No. of Suites: 112
Services and Amenities: Valet service, Garage and parking, Car hire, Laundry, Complimentary shoeshine, Baby-sitting service, Complimentary airport transportation, Complimentary newspaper, TV, Radio, Phone, Shampoo, Lotion, Soaps, Caps, Shoe mitt, Shoehorn
Restrictions: Small pets allowed; handicapped access to 8 suites
Concierge: 8:00 a.m.-10:00 p.m.
Room Service: 24 hours
Restaurant: The Hermitage Dining Room, 6:30-10:30 a.m., 11:00 a.m.-2:00 p.m., 6:00-10:00 p.m., Dress Code
Bar: Oak Bar & Veranda, 11:00 a.m.-1:00 a.m.
Business Facilities: Message center, Secretarial service, Translators, Copiers, Audio-visual
Conference Rooms: 3, capacity 250
Sports Facilities: Full health spa
Location: I-40 West, Exit Church Street turn left, 7th Ave. turn left, Union St. turn right, 6th Ave. turn right

The Hermitage, a downtown Nashville landmark just across the street from Tennessee's State Capitol, is one of the few remaining examples of the beaux arts architectural style. Originally built in 1909, The Hermitage has hosted five U.S. presidents as well as other notables including Al Jolsen, Jack Dempsey, Gene Autry and Billy Graham. Totally restored in 1981 to become an elegant all-suite hotel, it is now even more elegant.

The exquisite marble lobby, accented by brass fittings and oriental carpets, sets the stage for the hotel's outstanding accommodations and fine personal service. The ballroom, with an intricately carved Russian walnut ceiling, is lovely.

Each guest suite's separate living room and bedroom are decorated in a choice of traditional, contemporary or oriental styles. The "traditional," with blue carpeting, wallpapers and draperies is most requested. The living room contains a built-in wet bar for gracious entertaining. Amenities include nightly turn-down service, complimentary newspaper, and lots of complimentary toiletries.

Throughout the richly panelled Hermitage dining room one can see the fine workmanship of master craftsmen brought over from Germany. The continental cuisine features such delicacies as tournedos Biarritz and fettucine Carolina. Live entertainment appears nightly.

MANSION ON TURTLE CREEK

Address: 2821 Turtle Creek Blvd., Dallas 75219
Phone No.: 214-559-2100
Toll-free Cable: US 800-527-5432, TX 800-442-3408
Reservation Services: Preferred Hotels, Leading Hotels, 800-323-7500
Rates: $$$*
Credit Cards: All major credit cards
No. of Rooms: 143 **Suites:** 14
Services and Amenities: Valet service, Laundry, Garage and parking, Car hire, Currency exchange, Complimentary shoeshine, House doctor, Baby-sitting service, Complimentary newspaper, Cable TV, Radio, Bath Phone, Robes, Specially packaged bath products
Restrictions: Small pets (deposit required); handicapped access to 1 room
Concierge: 24 hours
Room Service: 24 hours
Restaurant: The Mansion on Turtle Creek Restaurant, Dress Code except Sat.-Sun. before 5:00 p.m.
Bar: The Mansion Bar, Mon.-Thur. 11:30 a.m.-1:00 a.m., Fri.-Sat. 11:30 a.m.-2:00 a.m., Sun. Noon-Midnight
Business Facilities: Message center, Secretarial service, Copiers, Audio-visual, other services arranged by concierge
Conference Rooms: 7, capacity 15-200
Sports Facilities: Swimming pool
Location: 30 min. from Dallas/Ft. Worth airport, 15 min. from Love Field
Attractions: Near Highland Park Shopping Center, art galleries, boutiques, central business district

The internationally renowned Mansion on Turtle Creek was the first of the wonderful Rosewood Hotels. The historic Mediterranean-style mansion, secluded within 4.6 acres of landscaped grounds, is only 5 minutes from Dallas' central business district.

The entrance foyer—a 32-foot-high rotunda with arched windows—sets the tone for the opulent interiors designed by James Northcutt/ Hirsch Bedner and Associates.

All guest rooms are large, luxuriously comfortable and well-appointed. The furnishings are traditional and the art is original. French doors open onto individual balconies or private patios. Though all 14 suites vie for superiority, the 1200-square-foot Terrace Suite, with its spectacular skyline view of Dallas, is truly incomparable.

The restaurant and bar occupy the original Sheppard King Mansion. In the main restaurant, a fireplace at each end and museum quality art on the walls create a grand ambience. Our recent dinner there began with Louisiana crab cakes in a sauce of oysters and smoked peppers; then beefsteak tomatoes with Dallas mozzarella and avocado in a basil vinaigrette; roast Iowa lamb with artichoke tarragon sauce and wild mushrooms; and for dessert, white chocolate mousse in a tulip shell with raspberry sauce.

The Promenade Dining Room serves not only breakfast and lunch but also a quite fashionable high tea from 3 to 5 p.m. In the bar, the environment is like that of a most exclusive club: dark wood floor, low-beamed ceiling, forest green fabric walls and 18th-Century hunting paintings and lithographs.

Management and staff join in a sincere effort to provide the most enjoyable possible atmosphere for the guests. The hotel offers extensive facilities for business and pleasure while creating a special, memorable warmth.

STEPHEN F. AUSTIN HOTEL

Built in 1924 in the Renaissance Revival style, The Stephen F. Austin Hotel has been renovated to blend traditional elegance with contemporary ease. The downtown location on "The Avenue"—Austin's chic Congress Avenue, that is—is convenient to Texas' state capitol.

Quite large rooms featuring king-size canopy beds are available in a choice of several color schemes.

Dining in the Remington Room means fine American and continental cuisine served in gracious surroundings. A recent dinner began with an orange galantine of duck, fresh scallops with watercress mousseline and beurre blanc, and pink linguine with fresh asparagus tips. A veal chop Normande was the entree. The dessert, Gateau St. Honore, was exquisite. The hotel prides itself on its wine list.

The lobby lounge is a great place to relax with the house special drink, Kir Royale, to the strains of piano and harp music.

Guests are extended privileges to the Supreme Court Racquetball Club.

The hotel's concierge desk is open at every hour of the day and night to assist you, and every thought is given to making your stay at the Stephen F. Austin Hotel an exceptionally pleasant one.

Address: 710 Congress Avenue, Austin 78701
Phone No.: 512-476-1061
Telex: 767101
Rates: $$*
Credit Cards: AmEx, Visa, MC, DC, CB
No. of Rooms: 171 **Suites:** 14
Services and Amenities: Sundries available, Hand lotion, Shampoo, Vitabath, Sewing kit
Restrictions: Pets by arrangement; no handicapped access
Concierge: 24 hours
Room Service: 24 hours
Restaurant: The Remington, lunch and dinner; The Austin Garden Room, breakfast and lunch; Dress Code
Bar: Lobby Lounge, 11:00 a.m.-2:00 a.m.
Conference Rooms: 5, capacity 750
Location: Downtown, 5 mi. from airport, 5 blocks from major highway
Attractions: Club and restaurant area, Capitol building, Mt. Bonnell, Barton Springs

HOTEL CRESCENT COURT

Address: 400 Crescent Court, Dallas 75201
Phone No.: 214-871-3200
Toll-free Cable: 800-654-6541
Telex: 275555
Reservation Service: Preferred Hotels, 800-323-7500
Rates: $$*
Credit Cards: All major credit cards
No. of Rooms: 218 **Suites:** 28
Services and Amenities: Valet service, Laundry, Garage and parking, Car hire, Currency exchange, Complimentary shoeshine, Babysitting service, Cable TV, Radio, Bath phone, Robes, Lancaster bath products
Restrictions: Small pets allowed; handicapped access to 3 rooms
Concierge: 24 hours
Room Service: 24 hours
Restaurant: Beau Nash and Conservatory, Dress Code
Bar: Beau Nash Bar, Mon.-Fri. 11:30 a.m.-1:00 a.m., Sat.-Sun. Noon-1:30 a.m.
Business Facilities: Message center, Copiers, Audio-visual, Teleconferencing, Telex, Executive Conference Center accommodates any business requests
Conference Rooms: 11, capacity 10-300
Sports Facilities: Swimming pool. The Spa at Crescent is a Lancaster Beauty Farm
Location: 3 min. from downtown, 40 min. from Dallas/Ft. Worth Airport, 15 min. from Love Field
Attractions: Hotel is center of the Crescent Project; boutiques, art galleries, antique shops

Newly built by Rosewood, Inc., in 1985 on a 10½ acre site, the architectural style of the Hotel Crescent Court is nineteenth century Texas with a European traditional flair, featuring courtyards, fountains and ornamental iron work.

Original works of art are displayed in the Great Hall, a two-story vaulted room with oversized French windows and comfortable earth-toned furnishings. Dallasites gather here to enjoy continental breakfast, lunch, afternoon tea and cocktails.

The hotel is residential in character throughout, reminiscent of the finest homes. Spacious guest rooms have sitting areas, fresh greenery and furnishings that are beautiful as well as comfortable. The baths are clad in marble and stocked with the finest soaps and bath products.

The Beau Nash restaurant is done in the style of an Old World brasserie, with an open kitchen in which diners can see the wood-burning ovens and charcoal grills.

Dinner might begin with calamari in a special tomato-garlic sauce, followed by vegetable soup with cheese ravioli and, as an entree, grilled red snapper with fresh herbs and lemon butter, or linguini with sundried tomatoes and goat cheese seasoned with garlic and basil. For dessert, passion fruit cheesecake.

The Crescent Court is a mainstream business hotel, fully equipped for conferences of all sizes. A swimming pool and full health spa are on the premises. The hub location is most convenient; yet what a delight to come home after a long day's work to the gracious style and service of one of America's premier hotels.

MELROSE HOTEL

Built in 1924 and grandly re-opened in 1985, the Melrose stands as a venerable Dallas landmark. As you step from the circular drive bordered by stately palms into the marble-floored lobby, you will find yourself surrounded by comfortable elegance.
Guest rooms combine the feel of a gracious country estate with the amenities of a modern world class hotel.
The art deco style Garden Court restaurant offers the best Sunday brunch in Dallas. Afternoon tea is served here daily. Dinner features such house specialties as steak Melrose, Tommoso's pasta and apple Charlotte. The Library Bar entertains with vocalist and piano music in a setting modeled after an English country estate library.
Guests are extended privileges to The Centrum, a full service sporting facility, directly across the street.
The hotel's motto, "A landmark hotel marked by its style," is most appropriate to this fine example of a classic hotel marvelously reborn.

Address: 3015 Oaklawn Avenue, Dallas 75219
Phone No.: 214-521-5151
Toll-free Cable: 800-635-7673, 800-527-1488
Rates: $*
Credit Cards: DC, AmEx, Visa, MC, CB
No. of Rooms: 185 **Suites:** 21
Services and Amenities: Valet service, Car hire, Complimentary airport transportation, International currency exchange, Complimentary shoeshine, Baby-sitting service, Garage and parking only upon request, Laundry, Complimentary newspaper, Cable TV, Radio, Phone, Robes, 2 deluxe soaps, Shampoo, Conditioner, Lotion, Mouthwash, Sewing kit, Shoehorn, Toothbrush
Restrictions: Small pets accepted; handicapped access to 2 rooms
Concierge: 11:00 a.m.-7:00 p.m.
Room Service: 6:30 a.m.-Midnight
Restaurant: Garden Court, 6:30 a.m.-2:00 p.m., 6:30 p.m.-11:30 p.m., Dress Code
Bar: The Library piano bar, 11:00 a.m.-2:00 a.m.
Business Facilities: Message center, Secretarial service on call, Translators, Copiers, Audio-visual
Conference Rooms: 5, capacity 10-300
Location: Downtown, Love Field 2 min., DFW Regional 20 min., I-35/Stemmons Freeway 2 min.
Attractions: Dallas Theatre Center, Dallas Market Center, The Centrum health facility across the street

STOCKYARDS HOTEL

Address: 109 East Exchange Street, Ft. Worth 76106
Phone No.: 817-625-6427
Toll-free Cable: 800-423-8471
Rates: $*
Credit Cards: All major credit cards
No. of Rooms: 52 **Suites:** 4
Services and Amenities: Valet service, Garage and parking, Laundry, Baby-sitting service, TV, Radio, Phone, Rose soap, Shampoo, Conditioner, Sewing kit, Artesia water
Restrictions: No pets; handicapped access to one room
Room Service: Sun.-Thur. 6:30 a.m.-10:00 p.m., Fri.-Sat., 6:30 a.m.-11:00 p.m.
Restaurant: Booger Red Restaurant, Sun.-Thur. 6:30 a.m.-10:00 p.m., Fri.-Sat. 6:30 a.m.-11:00 p.m.
Bar: Booger Red Saloon
Business Facilities: Secretarial service available on request Mon.-Fri.
Conference Rooms: 3, capacity 15-150
Location: In center of historic stockyards district; from airport 183 to 820 to Stockyards area
Attractions: Walking distance to Billy Bob's Texas, cattle sales, western-related shopping

Smack-dab in the middle of Fort Worth's Stockyards Historic District, this 1907 hotel has been dramatically restored by architect Ward Bogard. As an immense oak door opens onto the grand lobby, you are greeted by architecture and decor that can only be described as "Cattle Baron Baroque," with large leather chesterfield sofas and carved wooden chairs bearing the hotel's longhorn steer emblem and upholstered with longhorn hide.

The 52 rooms share four different decorative motifs: Indian, Mountain Man, Victorian and Western. Rams' head lamps and 200-year-old wormwood shutters that open to lace curtains remind you that you are deep in the heart of Texas.

The Booger Red restaurant specializes in (surprise!) Texas cuisine, featuring the house specialty, a 20-ounce Porterhouse steak, aged to perfection and cooked to order. If you still have room, don't miss the praline cheesecake. Saddle-topped barstools set the tone in the Booger Red Saloon, where Happy Hour is a Fort Worth tradition.

There are also 3 meeting rooms, the largest of which will accommodate 150 persons.

This hotel offers its guests a glimpse back into the cattle drive days on the Chisholm Trail. And, although many of the hotels in this guide have famous names in their guest registers, this is the only one we know of that can claim, "Bonnie and Clyde slept here"; a gun carried by the bank-robbing duo is displayed on the lobby wall.

THE REMINGTON

Address: 1919 Briar Oaks Lane, Houston 77027
Phone No.: 713-840-7600
Telex: 765-536
Rates: $$$*
Credit Cards: Visa, MC, AmEx, DC, CB
No. of Rooms: 248 **Suites:** 27
Services and Amenities: Valet service, Laundry, Gift shop, Garage and parking, Car hire, Complimentary shoeshine, Baby-sitting service, Complimentary newspaper, Cable TV, Phone in bath, Radio, Robes, Whirlpool, Complimentary Gucci toiletries
Restrictions: No pets; handicapped access to 2 rooms
Concierge: 24 hours
Room Service: 24 hours
Restaurant: Garden Room/Conservatory, 6:30-11:00 a.m., 11:30 a.m.-2:00 p.m., 6:00-11:00 p.m., Dress Code
Bar: Bar & Grill, 11:00 a.m.-2:00 a.m.
Business Facilities: Message center, Secretarial service, Translators, Copiers, Audio-visual, Teleconferencing, Telex, Complete business center
Conference Rooms: 6, capacity 1-300
Sports Facilities: Jogging track across street, heated lap pool
Attractions: Galleria shopping within 2 mi., theatre district within 5 mi., limousine transportation available

The Remington is situated on three heavily wooded acres in Houston's prestigious Galleria and River Oaks area. The 12-story Bauhaus style exterior was designed by the architectural firm of Shepherd, Boyd of Dallas. The lobby, by Los Angeles interior decorator Louis Cataffo, is among the world's most beautiful and the rest of the hotel follows in grand style.

The rooms are large and comfortably furnished. Bed linens are 100% cotton; pillows are goose down; floor-to-ceiling windows bring the outside in. The baths gleam with brass fixtures, marble and travertine, and are provided with terry cloth robes and designer toiletries. Only the finest fabrics and materials have been used throughout. The suites rival the finest residences for graciousness. Though no two are alike, all share the feeling of genuine opulence one has come to expect in a Rosewood hotel.

The Garden Room/Conservatory, with its hand stencilled walls and antique French tapestries, blends formal design with a pastorale view of the Post Oak Park. An appetizer of grilled marinated roast quail on panfried ancho chili pasta sets the stage for the restaurant's most celebrated entree, black bass with scallion, garlic vinaigrette. For dessert, the chocolate marjolaine is unbeatable. The Bar at the Remington is Houston's most "in" spot. Polished hand-rubbed travertine highlights a clublike atmosphere of big-city sophistication and world class luxury.

This is a quintessential newly built hotel, conceived all of a piece and realized without thought of expense to provide an experience guests will treasure and return to time and again.

THE LANCASTER

In the busiest part of downtown Houston, the Lancaster Hotel provides an oasis of quiet charm and European style elegance. The soothing interiors are done in the style of an English country manor house, and fine art abounds.

The guest rooms feature a burgundy, green and cream color scheme, with custom chintz-covered furnishings and large plants. Each room has three or four telephones. The palatial bathrooms feature Italian marble floors and vanities, all brass fittings, oversized towels, fresh flowers and a bountiful selection of toiletries. Of the eight suites, The Presidential is most outstanding: original paintings grace the walls, a Persian rug covers the floor, and the ceilings are twelve feet high.

The Lancaster Grille, its clublike atmosphere highlighted by the English hunting scene paintings that bedeck every bit of available wall space, is intimate and inviting. The menu changes seasonally, emphasizing continental cuisine and fresh ingredients. The Grille provides 24-hour room service to guests.

Guests to whom physical fitness is a priority enjoy privileges at the Texas Club.

Old-fashioned traditions of courtesy, personalized service and warm hospitality live on at the Lancaster. For lovers of the arts, Alley Theatre and Jones Hall, home of the Houston Ballet, are across the street; and visitors have remarked that the hotel itself rivals most museums.

Address: 701 Texas Avenue, Houston 77002
Phone No.: 713-228-9500
Toll-free Cable: 800-231-0336
Telex: 790-506
Reservation Services: SRS, 800-223-5652
Rates: $$$*
Credit Cards: AmEx, Visa, MC, DC, CB
No. of Rooms: 93 **Suites:** 8
Services and Amenities: Sundries at concierge station, Valet service, Garage and parking, Complimentary shoeshine, Laundry, Complimentary newspaper, TV, Radio, Phone, Robes, Soap, Conditioner, Lotion, Sewing kit, Shower cap
Restrictions: No pets; handicapped access to 6 rooms
Concierge: 7:00 a.m.-Midnight
Room Service: 24 hours
Restaurant: Lancaster Grille, 6:30 a.m.-Midnight; Charley's 517, Mon.-Fri. 11:00 a.m.-2:30 p.m., daily 6:00 p.m.-Midnight, Dress Code
Bar: Grille, 11:00 a.m.-Midnight
Business Facilities: Message center, Secretarial service, Translators, Copiers, Audio-visual, Telex
Conference Rooms: 3, capacity 50
Sports Facilities: Handball/squash court, health club, aerobics, full health spa, whirlpool, sauna, massage, weight training
Location: Downtown theatre district, ½ mi. from major highway
Attractions: NASA, Astrodome, Astro Domain, Houston Zoo, museums, art galleries

STEIN ERIKSEN LODGE

Address: P.O. Box 3779, Park City 84060
Phone No.: 801-649-3700
Toll-free Cable: 800-453-1302
Rates: $*
Credit Cards: All major credit cards
No. of Rooms: 120 **Suites:** 50
Services and Amenities: Gift shop, Parking, Car hire, Baby-sitting service, Laundry, Game area, Complimentary newspaper, Cable TV, Radio, Phone, Robes, Whirlpool bath, Shampoo, Conditioners, Lip balm, Lip brush
Restrictions: No pets; handicapped access to all rooms
Concierge: 24 hours
Room Service: Twice daily
Restaurant: Glitretind Gourmet Room, hours depend on season; Birkebeiner Restaurant
Bar: Troll Hallen Lounge
Business Facilities: Audio-visual, Teleconferencing, Copiers, Secretarial service arranged on request
Conference Rooms: 3, capacity 180
Sports Facilities: Skiing, golf, tennis, fishing, riding, hot air ballooning, full health spa
Location: Mountains-East on I-80 to 224 South, 30 mi. Airport-E. on I-80 to 224 South, 40 mi., 224 South to Park City
Attractions: Art galleries, scenic ride on steam locomotive, Summer Shakespeare Festival, writers conference, hot air balloon ride

You can ski to Deer Valley's chairlifts right from the doorstep of this rustic Norwegian style lodge high in the Rocky Mountains. A skiers' paradise, the Lodge is truly world class, and no wonder—it is the pride and joy of 1952 Olympic Gold Medalist Stein Eriksen. Warmth pervades the Lodge from the lobby with its beamed cathedral ceiling, giant fieldstone fireplace and grand piano, to the extra-cozy guest rooms. Spectacular mountain scenery is seen from every window and balcony. The furnishings are hand-carved and the fabrics imported.

Each large guest room is ultra-comfortable in the best Scandinavian tradition. The baths have separate dressing and bathing areas, over-sized towels, whirlpool, gold-plated fixtures, telephone, robe, complimentary toiletries and more.

When the snow melts from the slopes, a wide range of year-round activities are available. The lodge has full health spa facilities. Guests are extended privileges at nearby Park Meadows Country club, with its golf course designed by Jack Nicklaus, indoor and outdoor tennis, racquetball and swimming. The surrounding mountains are ideal for hiking, and horseback riding, bicycling, windsurfing, fishing and hot air ballooning adventures can be arranged through the concierge.

In the short time it has been open, Stein Eriksen Lodge has been discovered by a growing number of American and European vacationers who appreciate the finest in mountain resort accommodations.

THE EQUINOX

Since this inn first opened in 1769, it has played host to American Revolution leader Ethan Allen, Mrs. Abraham Lincoln and four U.S. Presidents. Now an official National Landmark, The Equinox re-opened in July 1985 after an elegant renovation directed by interior designer Carleton Varney.

This full service resort encompasses 22 acres (not counting the golf course) with extensive gardens, surrounded by the Taconic and Green Mountain ranges.

Many of the public rooms display murals by American painters depicting United States historical events. The New England style guest rooms feature armoires, wing chairs and an individualized decor using fine quality reproductions. The suites have genuine Early American antiques.

The spacious main dining room, done in warm pastel colors with a vaulted ceiling and large windows looking out onto Equinox Mountain, serves exquisite cuisine. A springtime dinner began with Escargot in puff pastry, accompanied by Freemark Abbey Chardonnay, and a light salad of fresh greens. The entree was rack of lamb in sauce Beaujolais with mint chutney on the side, accompanied by a Chateau Leoville Payferre. For dessert, a fresh banana Gateau.

The less formal March Tavern serves light fare in an authentic Early American setting; the windows afford a view of the classic New England village green.

The Equinox provides a unique setting ideal for business conferences. Five meeting rooms offer complete facilities including computerized audio-visual equipment.

There is activity aplenty for everybody, with an 18-hole PGA golf course, five tennis courts lighted for night play, a swimming pool and some of the best cross-country and downhill skiing in the Northeast. The area also offers theatre, art museums, historical sites, and great shopping.

Address: P.O. Box 46, Route 7A, Manchester Village 05254
Phone No.: 802-362-4700
Toll-free Cable: 800-362-4747
Reservation Services: Horizon Group Res., 800-351-5656
Rates: $*
Credit Cards: All major credit cards
No. of Rooms: 154 **Suites:** 16
Services and Amenities: Gift shop, Valet service, Parking, Car hire, Complimentary shoeshine, Baby-sitting service, Game area, Laundry, Telephone, TV
Restrictions: No pets; handicapped access to 2 rooms
Concierge: All day
Room Service: All day
Restaurant: Main Dining Room, 7:00-10:00 a.m., Noon-2:30 p.m., 6:00-10:00 p.m.; Marsh Tavern Buffet, Noon-2:30 p.m. except Sun., 6:00-10:00 p.m., Dress Code
Bar: Marsh Tavern, Noon-12:30 a.m.
Business Facilities: Message center, Secretarial service, Copiers, Audio-visual, Telex
Conference Rooms: 5, capacity 5-225
Sports Facilities: 3 Har-tru, 2 clay tennis courts, 18-hole golf course, skiing, riding, paddle tennis, cross-country skiing
Location: Country, 1 mi. from Manchester Center, 30 mi. from Rutland Airport, 60 mi. from Albany Airport, 1 mi. from Route 7
Attractions: Hildene (Lincoln family estate) 1 mi. away, Stratton Bromley & Magic Mountains skiing 20-30 min., 35 shops 1 mi. away

TOPNOTCH AT STOWE

Address: P.O. Box 1260, Stowe 05672
Phone No.: 802-253-8585
Toll-free Cable: Eastern US 800-451-8686, Canada 800-228-8686
Rates: $
Credit Cards: All major credit cards inc. Discover
No. of Rooms: 90 **Suites:** 8
Services and Amenities: Gift shop, Laundry, Valet service, Library, Beauty shop, Garage and parking, Car hire, Currency exchange, Baby-sitting service, Cable TV, Radio, Hair dryers, Complimentary toiletries, Whirlpool bath for 2
Restrictions: Pets in rooms only; handicapped access to 5 rooms
Concierge: 8:00 a.m.-11:00 p.m. seasonal
Room Service: 8:30 a.m.-9:00 p.m.
Restaurant: Main Dining Room, 7:30 a.m.-10:30 p.m., Dress Code
Bar: Buttertub, 11:00 a.m.-2:00 a.m.
Business Facilities: Message center, Secretarial service, Translators, Copiers, Audio-visual, Teleconferencing, Telex
Conference Rooms: 5, capacity 10-225
Sports Facilities: Pool, 14 tennis courts, croquet, putting green, hiking, riding, skiing, ice skating, full health spa, fishing
Location: On mountain road, 4 mi. from downtown, 10 mi. from I-89; airport transport can be arranged from Stowe or Burlington
Attractions: Head Class tennis tournament, Mt. Mansfield, craft fairs, antique car ralley, sculpture gardens, formal gardens

Stowe is perhaps the most popular resort village in Vermont, and Topnotch offers the finest accommodations in Stowe. Home of the Head Classic Tennis Tournament each August, this 120-acre resort and conference center blends the charm and quality service of the finest European hotels with the friendly informality of a New England mountain lodge.

The large guest rooms, each uniquely decorated, are furnished with antique tables, chests and armoires. Every room has its own library and big comfortable leather-covered chairs in which to relax and enjoy the views. One notable suite can be expanded to seven bedrooms—perfect for a family get-together!

The main dining room is a Stowe tradition, and return visitors have their favorite dishes. You can't go wrong, though, with a pate de foie gras appetizer, Caesar salad made tableside, rack of lamb with Biarritz potatoes, and for dessert the sensational Baked Alaska.

Guests gather in the Buttertub Bar to enjoy the jazz ensemble and crackling fire. Afternoon tea is served in the Notch Room during the winter and on the terrace in summer. The poolside Gazebo Bar is another popular socializing spot.

Wander among the property's wooded hills, open meadows, mountain streams and brooks with their fine network of runners' trails, or enjoy privileges to the Racquet Club and health spa. The Topnotch Ski Touring Center, Equestrian Center and Stowe Country Club offer more sporting possibilities. Mt. Mansfield's famed ski slopes are just two miles away. Full conference facilities are available at The Conference Center at Topnotch, centrally located in nearby Stowe village.

WOODSTOCK INN

Rockresorts' ultimate New England country inn, newly built in 1969 on Woodstock's village green, epitomizes traditional colonial architecture. Hand-cut stone, weathered Vermont timbers, patchwork quilts and a ten-foot fireplace set the stage for a memorable resort experience. The Inn's 120 well appointed guest rooms are exceptionally spacious and comfortable.

The main dining room, Woodstock's premier gourmet rendezvous, offers such delights as beef wellington Wynia, named after renowned chef Peter Wynia, and chocolate Toblerone fondue. Sample their special drink, the Golden Eagle, in the elegantly rustic Pine Room Bar.

Skiing, of course, is Woodstock's claim to fame (the first ski tow in the United States was built here in 1934). The Woodstock Inn operates the Suicide Six ski slopes, three miles from the Inn, and Woodstock Ski Touring Center with nearly fifty miles of mountain trails. Sleigh rides, ice skating and dogsledding are also available. Activities abound in the spring and summer as well. Visit the maple syrup sugarhouse; enjoy the heated pool, ten outdoor and two indoor tennis courts, four handball and squash courts and the Robert Trent Jones golf course; spend a day antiquing in the village or take a tour in the Inn's steam car. In autumn, even the finest sporting facilities cannot upstage the splendor of hillsides painted with blazing red and gold foliage.

tended privileges to the Quechee Country Club. In autumn, even the finest sporting facilities cannot upstage the splendor of hillsides painted with blazing red and gold foliage.

Unsurpassed accommodations and service amid traditional New England village charm make visiting this Rockresort an experience to remember.

Address: 14 The Green, Woodstock 05091
Phone No.: 802-457-1100
Rates: $
Credit Cards: AmEx, MC, Visa, CB, DC
No. of Rooms: 120 **Suites:** 2
Services and Amenities: Valet service, Garage and parking, Complimentary shoeshine, Laundry, Cable TV, Radio, Phone, Robes, Complimentary toiletries
Restrictions: No handicapped access
Concierge: 9:00 a.m.-5:00 p.m.
Room Service: 7:15 a.m.-11:00 p.m.
Restaurant: Main Dining Room, Noon-9:30 p.m., Dress Code; Coffee Shop 7:00 a.m.-11:00 a.m., Noon-5:00 p.m., 5:30-8:30 p.m.
Bar: Pine Room, 11:00 a.m.-Midnight
Business Facilities: Message center, Secretarial service, Copiers, Audio-visual
Conference Rooms: 6, capacity 300
Sports Facilities: 12 tennis courts, 4 handball courts, croquet, 18-hole golf course, skiing, full health spa, indoor sports center
Location: In the village
Attractions: Near Billings Farm Museum, Calvin Coolidge home, Queechee Gorge

COMMONWEALTH PARK

Address: 9th & Bank Street, Richmond 23219
Phone No.: 804-343-7300
Toll-free Cable: 800-343-7302
Reservation Services: 800-223-6800
Rates: $
Credit Cards: AmEx, DC, Visa, MC, CB
No. of Suites: 59
Services and Amenities: Valet service, Garage and parking, Car hire, Laundry, Baby-sitting service, TV, Mini-bar, Towel warmer, Phone in bath, Bidet, Robes, Complimentary toiletries
Restrictions: No pets; handicapped access to 2 rooms
Concierge: 7:00 a.m.-11:00 p.m.
Room Service: 24 hours
Restaurant: Assembly, 6:00 p.m.-10:30 p.m., Dress Code
Bar: Memories, 5:00 p.m.-2:00 a.m.
Business Facilities: Available upon advance request: Secretarial service, Copiers, Audio-visual, Message center
Conference Rooms: 2, capacity 12-50
Sports Facilities: Whirlpool, sauna, massage upon request, access to swimming pool and health club
Location: Downtown: Capitol Square near I-64 and I-95; airport transportation by reservation
Attractions: State Capitol and Governor's Mansion, James River Museum, shopping

This small, elegant all-suite hotel has been thoughtfully designed with the business traveller in mind, and the Capitol Square location couldn't be more convenient.

Each of the one- or two-bedroom suites is furnished with 18th Century mahogany reproductions and decorated with original museum prints. Subdued color schemes contribute to the fine residential feel. Rooms are provided with mini wet bars, and each has a dining table for four. The spacious marble baths feature towel warmers, bidets and telephones.

The Assembly Restaurant, seating only 48 persons, provides a rich red candlelit intimate retreat in which to dine on Dungeness crab Newburg, Dover sole and chocolate mousse cake, all accompanied by the finest wines. The Memories Lounge has music on the grand piano five nights a week.

The experienced staff makes a special point to provide each guest with individual attention, fulfilling the Commonwealth Park's "home away from home" credo.

RITZ-CARLTON

This elegant eight-story Federal style hotel on downtown Washington's Embassy Row has recently undergone a marvelous redecorating by Sister Parish of the famous Parish-Hadley Associates designer firm.

To call the guest rooms "plush" is an understatement. One is surrounded by homelike comforts—overstuffed sofas, the softest imported wool carpeting, multi-line telephones and dreamy bedtime chocolates to mention only a few.

The baths feature the finest imported European Emperor peach marble, with counter tops and vanities of red clay granite color coordinated to match, the whole artfully lit and reflected in mirrored walls. Fluffy terry robes and soft towels, heat lamps, a basket of fine English bath products and a telephone are among the many bath amenities.

The menu at the warm, inviting Jockey Club Restaurant is international in scope. Dinner might consist of prosciutto and melon, hearts of palm and the famous Jockey Club crab cake, all topped off by a raspberry souffle.

The Fairfax Bar, open until 2:00 a.m., has piano music in a comfortable setting of deep chintz chairs, slow-burning fireplace and wood panelling.

Within walking distance of the best of Washington D.C., the Ritz-Carlton measures up to the finest international tradition of small, elegant, professionally staffed hotels.

Address: 2100 Massachusetts Avenue N.W., Washington DC 20008

Phone No.: 202-835-2100
Toll-free Cable: 800-424-8008
Telex: 26378 Ritz UR

Rates: $$$*

Credit Cards: MC, Visa, AmEx, DC

No. of Rooms: 240 **Suites:** 30

Services and Amenities: Valet service, Garage and parking, Complimentary shoeshine, Laundry, House doctor, Baby-sitting service, Phone with 2 lines, 2 Phones in each room, Complimentary newspaper, TV, Radio, Robes, Soaps

Restrictions: Handicapped access to 2 rooms

Concierge: 7:00 a.m.-11:00 p.m.

Room Service: 24 hours

Restaurant: The Jockey Club, 6:30 a.m.-10:30 p.m., Dress Code

Bar: The Fairfax Bar, 11:30 a.m.-2:00 a.m.

Business Facilities: Secretarial service, Copiers, Audio-visual, Telex

Conference Rooms: 6 theatre-style, 30-290 capacity

Location: 7 mi., 15 min. from airport

Attractions: Within walking distance of monuments, shopping in Georgetown

THE HAY-ADAMS

Address: One Lafayette Square, Washington D.C. 20006
Phone No.: 202-638-6600
Toll-free Cable: 800-424-5054
Telex: TWX 710-822-9543
Reservation Services: Steigenberger Reservation, 800-223-5652
Rates: $$*
Credit Cards: AmEx, MC, Visa, DC, CB, Eurocard, JCB
No. of Rooms: 155 **Suites:** 21
Services and Amenities: Valet service, Garage and parking, Car hire, Currency exchange, Laundry, Complimentary shoeshine, Baby-sitting service, Bath phone, Robes, Crabtree & Evelyn shampoo, Bath lotion, 2 soaps, Sewing kit, Shoe cloth, Shower caps, Shoehorn, Color TV, Complimentary newspaper, Radio
Restrictions: Small dogs; handicapped access to 50 rooms
Concierge: 7:00 a.m.-Midnight
Room Service: 24 hours; also Butler service
Restaurant: The John Hay Room, Noon-2:30 p.m., 6:00-11:00 p.m., Dress Code; Adams Room, 6:30 a.m.-2:30 p.m.; English Grill, Noon-11:00 p.m.
Bar: John Hay Lounge, Noon-Midnight, English Grill, Noon-11:00 p.m.
Business Facilities: Secretarial service, Copiers, Telex; Arrangements can be made for other business services
Conference Rooms: 4, capacity 35 to 140
Attractions: White House, Capitol, ten museums, Mt. Vernon, Georgetown, five universities, Potomac River

Directly across from the White House, this stunning grand hotel styles itself "an island of civility in a sea of power." An epicenter of Washington high society since 1927, the Hay-Adams has welcomed among its many notable guests Charles Lindbergh, Amelia Earhart, Sinclair Lewis and Ethel Barrymore.

The facade, by the legendary architect Mirhan Mesrobian, is pure Italian Renaissance. The lobby strives for—and surpasses—the ambience of a grand manor home with its lofty ceilings, dazzling chandeliers, richly polished walnut, English antiques and fine 17th Century Medici tapestry.

Each guest room is individually furnished with fine antique reproductions and sensuous fabric textures. The spacious marble-clad baths offer every amenity, including hair dryers, telephones, hand mirrors and sumptuous five-foot towels. Several rooms have fireplaces and balconies affording views of the White House, Lafayette Square and the Washington Monument. A corner suite, overlooking the White House grounds, features a fully equipped kitchen, dining area, four poster bed, three closets and a lovely dressing table.

Fine dining is to be had in the John Hay Room, whose English country estate atmosphere is an ideal environment in which to enjoy a feast of Beluga caviar, heart of palm in raspberry vinaigrette and Chateaubriand with truffles. The wine cellar is most exceptional.

The sun-drenched Adams Room is the setting for many a Washington "power breakfast," as well as afternoon tea served in intimate alcoves.

The assistance of a full concierge staff exemplifies the extraordinary level of personal service, attentive but never overbearing, that keeps guests returning year after year.

JEFFERSON HOTEL

Address: 16th & M Street N.W., Washington DC 20036
Phone No.: 202-347-2200
Toll-free Cable: 800-368-5966
Telex: 258879
Reservation Services: 800-223-6800
Rates: $$$*
Credit Cards: All major credit cards
No. of Rooms: 102 **Suites:** 30
Services and Amenities: Valet service, Garage and parking, Car hire, Currency exchange, Laundry (hand-ironed), Complimentary shoeshine, House doctor, Baby-sitting service, Complimentary newspaper, Cable TV, Radio, Telephone, Robes, Complimentary toiletries
Restrictions: Pets limited; handicapped access to 3 rooms
Concierge: 24 hours
Room Service: 24 hours
Restaurant: Hunt Club, 6:30 a.m.-11:00 p.m., Dress Code
Bar: Hunt Club Lounge, 11:00 a.m.-2:00 a.m.
Business Facilities: Translators, Copiers, Audio-visual, Teleconferencing, Telex
Conference Rooms: 2, capacity 75
Sports Facilities: Health club facilities available at YMCA
Location: Downtown Washington, 4 blocks to White House
Attractions: Near historic Washington DC, Georgetown shopping, 3 blocks to Metro, near National Geographic Building

Returning guests describe this venerable grand hotel in a single word: "home." Indeed, The Jefferson has been known for impeccable service and Old World charm ever since it opened its doors in 1925. Many visitors to Washington D.C. stay here year after year; they have their favorite rooms, and the staff greets them by name. Each extraordinarily large guest room is luxuriously appointed, no two alike. The furnishings are predominantly 18th Century Georgian in style, with four-poster beds, grandfather clocks, Scalamandre fabrics and many English and French Empire antiques. The baths have marble countertops, large mirrors and plentiful French and English bath amenities. Guests are also treated to fresh flowers, hand-ironed laundry, imported English tea baskets and the full service of a concierge and night porter.

The Hunt Club provides a warm atmosphere for intimate dining. Such house specialties as shrimp Dubois, steak au poivre, Belgian endive and watercress salad with hazelnut dressing, and desserts like white chocolate mousse or Bete Noir with sauce Anglaise make for a memorable meal.

The Hunt Club Lounge, with its English country house library atmosphere and intimate alcoves, is a perfect spot in which to linger. You may wish to try the house drink, vouvray with crushed strawberries. Explorers Hall, headquarters of the National Geographic Society, is across the street, and the White House and Smithsonian Institute are within easy walking distance.

SORRENTO HOTEL

Past the sparkling Italian fountain, one is admitted by the doorman from the entrance *porte cochere* into a lobby richly panelled in handcrafted Honduras mahogany. An intimate ambience aglow with warm subtle colors and textures characterizes this newly-remodeled 1908 hotel.

The beautifully furnished guest rooms contain many antiques. Beds are made up with all-cotton sheets and goose down pillows. Special touches such as twice-daily maid service and evening turndown with a chocolate will make you feel pampered.

Almost half the hotel's guest accommodations are suites, including two penthouses. The largest, 3,000 square feet with a baby grand piano, a fireplace, a library, and a terrace overlooking the city and Puget Sound, is the finest hotel room in Seattle.

Begin your morning with a complimentary Wall Street Journal. Enjoy privileges at the Seattle Club, a prestigious downtown athletic club. Later, join other guests who gather daily in the Fireside Lounge for afternoon tea in the English manner.

The Hunt Club restaurant, with its rose and salmon color scheme and romantic atmosphere, serves the bounty of the Northwest, and particularly its fine seafood, with true continental flair. Assorted smoked fish and shellfish, warm quail salad, fresh Northwest salmon with yellow bell pepper and basil sauce, and a fresh fruit Napoleon are among delights that await you.

Address: 900 Madison Street, Seattle 98104
Phone No.: 206-622-6400
Toll-free Cable: 800-426-1265
Telex: 244206 SORRUR
Reservation Services: Preferred Hotels
Rates: $*
Credit Cards: AmEx, MC, Visa, DC
No. of Rooms: 76 **Suites:** 32
Services and Amenities: Sundries available at front desk, Valet service, Laundry, Garage and parking, Car hire, Complimentary shoeshine, Baby-sitting service, Florist, Complimentary Wall Street Journal, Cable TV, Audio cassette player, Phone, Robes, Shampoo, Conditioner, Bath gel, 2 soaps
Restrictions: No pets; no handicapped access
Concierge: 24 hours
Room Service: 6:00 a.m.-Midnight
Restaurant: The Hunt Club, breakfast, lunch and dinner
Bar: Hunt Club Lounge & Fireside Lounge, until 2:00 a.m. daily
Business Facilities: Message center, Secretarial service, Copiers, Audio-visual, Teleconferencing, Telex
Conference Rooms: 2 theatre-style, capacity 80; conference-style, capacity 18
Location: Downtown, 15 mi. north of airport, I-5 to Madison & James St. Exit, ¼ mi. from I-25
Attractions: Close to Puget Sound waterfront where harbor tours, excursions and ferries to scenic islands are available; one hour from Cascade Range, 1½ hrs. from Mt. Rainier

ALEXIS HOTEL

Address: 1007 First Avenue at Madison, Seattle 98104
Phone No.: 206-624-4844
Toll-free Cable: 800-426-7033
Rates: $$
Credit Cards: AmEx, Visa, CB, DC, MC, JCB
No. of Rooms: 54 **Suites:** 24
Services and Amenities: Parfumerie, Bookstore, Valet service, Laundry, Garage and parking, Complimentary shoeshine, Baby-sitting service, Complimentary newspaper, Cable TV, Phone in bath, Radio, Robes, Shampoo, Lotion, Cologne, Bath gel
Restrictions: Small pets with deposit; handicapped access to 3 rooms
Concierge: 24 hours
Room Service: 6:30 a.m.-Midnight
Restaurant: Alexis Restaurant, 6:30 a.m.-10:30 p.m.; The Mark Tobey Pub, 11:30 a.m.-11:00 p.m.
Bar: The Bar, 11:00 a.m.-1:30 a.m.
Business Facilities: Message center, Secretarial service, Translators, Copiers, Audio-visual
Conference Rooms: 2, capacity 75
Sports Facilities: 2 rooftop asphalt tennis courts
Location: Downtown, 13 mi. from airport on I-5 North, 5 blocks from major highway
Attractions: Waterfront Place: 6 blocks of shops and services; 4 blocks to Pioneer Square and Pike Place Farmers Market

In the historic Waterfront Place district midway between Pike Street Market and Pioneer Square, this 1901 hotel listed on the National Register of Historic Places is a centerpiece of Seattle's fascinating downtown restoration. The outer shell has been preserved, while the interior has been redone in sophisticated European style.

Each guest is treated to special personalized services such as a small bottle of sherry and a warm welcome upon arrival, use of the hotel's steam room (guaranteeing a restful night's sleep), nightly turndown service, complimentary shoeshine and continental breakfast served alongside one's choice of morning newspapers.

Each of the 54 guest rooms, almost half of them suites, is beautifully decorated with antique tables, overstuffed chairs, brass reading lamps and cable TV concealed in an armoire. The dramatic baths feature black tile, marble counters, luxurious linens and robes, telephones and abundant toiletries. Several suites have woodburning fireplaces and whirlpool baths.

The Alexis Restaurant has won a unique place in the hearts of Seattle residents. The decor—cane chairs, palm plants, fine china and crystal—sets the stage for the elegant cuisine. Selections from the wine cellar complement each dish to perfection. A recent five-course dinner included mousseline of sole and crab, Red currant ice, two lamb chops roasted as a rack with rosemary and elephant garlic, salad of seasonal greens with Zinfandel vinaigrette, and a dessert choice of cheese and fruit or chocolate French silk.

The bar, decorated in dark blues, peach and marble, plays host to those guests who wish to curl up and enjoy the famous house recipe for hot chocolate beside the fireplace.

For physical fitness enthusiasts, two rooftop tennis courts are available. Guests also enjoy privileges to the Seattle Club and Pacific Nautilus. A scenic jogging route along the Seattle waterfront starts at The Alexis' front door.

GRAN HOTEL EL CONVENTO

The final stop on our tour of America's most elegant small hotels has quite an unusual history. Gran Hotel El Convento began life as a Carmelite convent in 1651 and continued in that role for over two and one-half centuries. In 1959 Mr. Robert F. Woolworth purchased the building from the Catholic Church and commissioned a total renovation, realized by architect Luis Sifuentes and finally completed in 1983 to offer the finest accommodations in this, the nation's oldest major city.

The imposing Spanish architecture focuses on an enormous open courtyard fronted by classical arches and colonnades. The courtyard has a swimming pool and an extraordinary open air dining room, El Patio, serving international and Spanish cuisine. On most nights, there are flamenco shows, piano and guitar music under the stars.

The large rooms are charmingly decorated and offer such amenities as satellite TV, toiletries and in-room safe deposit boxes. The marvelous view of San Juan Harbor from the upper floors, and especially from the rooftop, is not to be missed.

In the very heart of old San Juan, you will be a short taxi ride from the airport and the several business areas. Should you desire, day trips can be arranged to most out-island destinations.

Address: 100 Cristo Street (P.O. Box 1048), San Juan 00902
Phone No.: 809-723-9020
Toll-free Cable: 800-468-2779
Telex: 3453199
Reservation Services: Utell/Provotel LRI, 800-223-0888
Rates: $
Credit Cards: Visa, MC, DC, AmEx, CB
No. of Rooms: 99 **Suites:** 5
Services and Amenities: Sundry shop, Garage and parking, Laundry, House doctor, Phone, Satellite TV, Toiletries, Shampoo, Rinse, Sewing kit
Restrictions: No pets; no handicapped access
Concierge: 8:00 a.m.-3:30 p.m.
Room Service: 7:00 a.m.-11:00 a.m.
Restaurant: El Patio, 7:00 a.m.-11:00 p.m.
Bar: Patio Bar, 11:00 a.m.-11:30 p.m.
Business Facilities: Message center, Copiers, Audio-visual, Telex
Conference Rooms: 6, capacity 50-300
Location: 25 min. from airport and major highway
Attractions: Museums, restaurants, stores, cultural attractions

PHOTO CREDITS

Jaime Ardiles-Arce (24, 25, 30, 31, 62, 88, 89, 106, 107, 109, 112, 113)
Brown (71)
Buchen & Company (13)
C. Cacioppo/Capt. Video (51 above)
Douglas DeFors (35)
Gifford Ewing (48)
Harron & Associates (76)
Gary Kufner (74)
Jane Lidz (18)
Frank Lotz Miller Photography Inc. (70)
Milroy/McAleer Inc. (75)
Moto Foto #7 (96)
F.P. Nagy (59)
Wayne Pearce (14)
Photo Graphics Inc. (118)
Karl H. Reichel (85)
Julius Shulman (20)
Simpson/Flint (121)
Sullivan Photo Service (72)
Paul Warchol (91)
Bob Ware (21)
Lawrence S. Williams Inc. (102)